THE
SAM-e
HANDBOOK

THE SAM-e HANDBOOK

The Fast, Natural Way to Overcome
Depression, Relieve the Pain of
Arthritis, Alleviate the Discomfort
of Fibromyalgia, and Boost
Your Energy

NANCY STEDMAN, M.S.

THREE RIVERS PRESS • NEW YORK

*To Dr. Murray Stedman, the first author in
my life*

Published by Three Rivers Press, 201 East 50th Street, New York, New
York 10022. Member of the Crown Publishing Group.

Random House, Inc. New York, Toronto, London, Sydney, Auckland
www.randomhouse.com

THREE RIVERS PRESS is a registered trademark of Random House, Inc.

Printed in the United States of America

Design by Susan Maksuta

Library of Congress Cataloging-in-Publication Data

Stedman, Nancy.
    The SAM-e handbook : the fast, natural way to overcome depression,
relieve the pain of arthritis, alleviate the discomfort of fibromyalgia, and
boost your energy / Nancy Stedman.—1st ed.
        p.   cm.
    Includes bibliographical references and index.
        1. Adenosylmethionine—Therapeutic use.   2. Arthritis—Alternative
treatment.   3. Fibromyalgia—Alternative treatment.   4. Depression,
Mental—Alternative treatment.   I. Title.

RM666.A278 S74   2000
615'.36—dc21   00-037430

ISBN 0-609-80654-8 (pbk.)

10 9 8 7 6 5 4 3 2 1

First Edition

CONTENTS

IMPORTANT NOTICE

This book is not intended to serve as a substitute for consultation with a qualified medical practitioner. If you have symptoms of any of the conditions described in *The SAM-e Handbook,* it is essential that you consult your doctor. This volume provides exciting information about SAM-e, but no book can replace the personal care that you require. As with any potent medicine, your doctor should be involved in your decision to use this supplement. Please note that SAM-e is not suitable for people who suffer from manic-depression.

The author has no financial interest in any producer or supplier of SAM-e.

ACKNOWLEDGMENTS

I would like to thank the many experts who shared their thoughts and research with me. They include Dr. Brian Berman, University of Maryland Medical School; Dr. Teodoro Bottiglieri, Baylor University's Institute for Metabolic Diseases; Dr. Steven Bratman, The Natural Pharmacy (TNP.com); author and physician Dr. Hyla Cass; Al Czap, *Alternative Medicine Review;* Marshall Fong, Pharmavite Corporation; Dr. Todd Henderson, Nutramax Laboratories; Dr. Bruce Kagan, University of California, Los Angeles School of Medicine; Dr. Charles Lieber, Alcohol Research and Treatment Center, Bronx Veterans Affairs Medical Center; Dr. José Maria Mato, University of Navarra, Pamplona, Spain; Dr. Ronald Moskowitz, Case Western Reserve University School of Medicine; and Dr. Lewis Opler, Columbia University College of Physicians and Surgeons.

I am indebted to the SAM-e users who told me their stories. Their names and identifying details have been altered to protect their privacy. I also wish to acknowledge the kind assistance of my agent, Sarah Jane Freyman, and my editor, Teryn Johnson. But most of all I would like to express my enduring gratitude to my husband, Steve Ditlea, who introduced me to SAM-e and helped in more ways than I could ever count.

ACKNOWLEDGMENTS

INTRODUCTION

The Fast, Natural Way to Relieve the Pain of Arthritis, Alleviate the Discomfort of Fibromyalgia, and Overcome Depression

An estimated 18 million Americans suffer from depression, some 21 million are disabled by arthritis, and 8 million by fibromyalgia, a little-understood debilitating condition in which muscles are achy and tired. Many Americans—most of them women—spend their days feeling uncomfortable. This doesn't have to happen. SAM-e (short for S-adenosylmethionine), a compound that appears naturally in the body, can lift the spirits of someone who is depressed, relieve the aching joints of osteoarthritis, and soothe the sore muscles of fibromyalgia. It works fast and produces no significant side effects.

Although it almost sounds too good to be true, SAM-e is much more than the supplement du jour. Unlike some compounds that have suddenly landed on health store shelves, seemingly out of nowhere, SAM-e was already backed by a great deal of solid science when it appeared on American shores. Clinical studies in Europe validate its effectiveness in relieving depression and arthritis. Additional research suggests that SAM-e may help those who suffer from fibromyalgia. Twenty years of experience in the fourteen industrialized countries that approve its use show that this natural substance is safe and easy to use.

American research has upheld its effectiveness, too. As long ago as 1987, a supplement to the *American Journal of Medicine* was devoted to SAM-e. More recently labs at Harvard Medical School, Baylor University Medical Center, and the University of California, Irvine, Medical Center, have delved into new uses of the compound. Even the normally conservative Arthritis Foundation issued a statement saying that SAM-e is effective for relieving pain. And the American Psychiatric Association, which is oriented toward prescription drugs, was intrigued enough about this antidepressant to invite a SAM-e expert to give a symposium on the subject at its 1999 annual meeting.

Many in the media are intrigued and often enthusiastic. In a story highlighted on its cover, *Newsweek* wrote, "Whatever the mechanism, there is little question that SAM-e can help fight depression." The *Los Angeles Times* said that "very few researchers dismiss its therapeutic potential." In early 2000, an episode of NBC's *Dateline* showcased a cheerful woman whose lifelong struggle with depression ended only after she began taking this nutraceutical.

Undeniably, SAM-e is hot. It is now impossible to walk by a health food store, vitamin shop, or drugstore without seeing a sign touting the supplement. One manufacturer estimates that at least one million American households, or about 1 percent of the total, already use SAM-e. The best-selling brand sold in excess of $60 million during the ten months it was available in 1999. Why are people buying SAM-e? Because it improves their well-being.

The SAM-e Handbook explains everything you need to know

about SAM-e: what it is, how it works, how to buy it, how to take it, and what results to expect. You will read about the experiences of people who were helped by the supplement. In this book, you will also learn about cutting-edge research that holds out the promise of treating devastating illnesses like liver disease. Most important of all, you will find out if SAM-e is right for you.

Chapter 1

HOW SAM-e CAN HELP YOU

Americans are taking back control of their health.

During the twentieth century, Western scientists were extraordinarily successful at wiping out many infectious diseases, at raising the level of public sanitation, at devising lifesaving operations and equipment, and at creating medications to treat a myriad of conditions. Today you can have a hand transplanted, your clogged arteries bypassed, your enlarged prostate shrunk, and your womb impregnated with septuplets. The pace of innovation has been breathtaking. Partly as a result, life expectancy in the United States almost doubled between the beginning and the end of the century.

But these impressive high-tech achievements have come at a cost. For starters, complicated medicine increases the chance of mistake, and an estimated 44,000 to 98,000 Americans die each year due to errors in medical treatment.[1] And when people live for a long time, chronic ailments become common. These problems—more threatening to the quality of life than to longevity—are often more difficult to treat than emergencies like heart attacks, which call out a full panoply of medical hardware. People with conditions like osteoarthritis spend years taking medicines that are fine in small doses but troublesome with long use.

Powerful mind-altering chemicals can create new difficulties. Those suffering from depression may experience such intense side effects from antidepressants that they prefer to live unmedicated and hence remain melancholic. And many people will consider surgery only as a last resort. Treatment plans that are acceptable to medical doctors may not be tolerable to their patients.

As a reaction against high-powered medicine, many Americans are seeking lower-tech alternatives with less potential for damage. Nearly one-half of the adult population relies on this gentler, less intrusive care, and the use of nutraceuticals (supplements made from natural sources), herbs, acupuncture, and body therapies is booming in the United States. Many patients are now educating their doctors, or at least inspiring them to educate themselves, about unfamiliar treatments. A growing number of insurance plans cover what is sometimes called alternative medicine. "Complementary medicine" is a more accurate moniker because studies in the United States show that unconventional therapies are most often used along with, rather than instead of, conventional treatment.

In March of 1999, an Italian pharmaceutical company did Americans a favor by introducing a twenty-year-old product called SAM-e onto the supplement market of the United States. Since then hundreds of thousands of Americans have discovered that the SAM-e molecule, which occurs naturally throughout the body, can relieve the pain of depression, arthritis, and fibromyalgia, a condition that is defined by muscles and intense fatigue.

SAM-e combines the best qualities of complementary and mainsteam medicine. Because S-adenosylmethionine (pronounced ess-add-eh-NO-sill-meth-I-uh-neen) is already present in the body, it is a low-tech nutraceutical that creates very few side effects and, for depression, works remarkably fast. But because it is classified as a prescription drug abroad, it has been well studied in a number of sophisticated clinical tests and certain brands are manufactured under the pristine conditions required for prescription medicine.

WHAT IS SAM-e?

Manufactured inside the body, SAM-e appears in most cells but is especially concentrated in the liver. S-adenosylmethionine results from the combination of the amino acid methionine (obtained from the diet through red meat and other animal products) and ATP (adenosine triphosphate), the body's main molecule for warehousing energy. Think of it as the Magic Johnson in a number of chemical relay teams. The ultimate team player, SAM-e sets off beneficial chain reactions, the most famous one known as methylation. Methylation, which occurs a billion times a second in our bodies, takes place when SAM-e "donates" its methyl group (a group of atoms) to another molecule. Both SAM-e and the recipient molecule become changed in the process. SAM-e can also be part of a process called transsulfuration, which involves the donation of sulfur and leads to, among other things, the production of a powerful antioxidant called glutathione.

When you take SAM-e as a supplement, you trigger some much-needed biochemical processes that protect cell membranes, regulate DNA, spark production of the shock-absorbing tissue in joints, and facilitate the movement of several brain chemicals that have been connected to depression. SAM-e benefits an usually wide range of ailments because methylation is related to an enormous number of body functions. Side effects are few because your body is already used to the substance.

Here is how one woman improved her well-being by taking SAM-e.

JANET'S STORY

The strains of a Viennese waltz wafted into her house, coming from somewhere far down her block. Suddenly Janet felt a surprising urge to get up and dance. "That's when I knew the black days were gone. During my depression, I couldn't stand to hear music—and I have adored music all my life," she says. The long depression had been hard on this forty-two-year-old full-time student and mother of two. Janet recalls, "Little things were big things; easily done things were impossible. I felt unloved, unwanted, and very unhappy."

The unhappiness seemed to come out of nowhere, just like the music. But the bleakness was not totally unfamiliar: Janet had experienced long-lasting depression a couple of times before, once after the birth of her second daughter. She had survived that period by taking a prescription antidepressant known as Elavil (chemical name amytriptyline). Although her sadness lifted, Janet almost felt as if she'd made a pact with the devil. As "punishment" for an improved mood, she was foggy, she had a constant dry mouth, and she could not enjoy sex with her husband.

Janet didn't know if she could tolerate such intense side effects again. Fortunately, her psychology professor referred her to a psychiatrist who prescribed the over-the-counter nutraceutical SAM-e. Within five days, Janet felt sunnier. She continued to ratchet up the dose a little each week, and within three weeks she knew that her depression had vanished.

About seven days later, Janet realized that she was also experiencing a totally unexpected benefit. Her hands, which had started to stiffen with the same osteoarthritis that had afflicted her mother, felt much more flexible. "I have always feared that I would have to give up crocheting, just as my mom did. But now it seems like I can crochet forever," Janet says. "SAM-e has truly given me back my life. I am able to do more and more and enjoy it better and better."

WHO WILL BENEFIT FROM USING SAM-e?

Like Janet, many people suffering from depression turn to SAM-e after being unhappy with other remedies. The biggest problem with conventional antidepressants is the side effects. Depending on the specific drug, people can experience headaches, dry mouth, low blood pressure, dangerously high blood pressure, weight gain, fogginess, anxiety, insomnia, and more. Worst of all for many are the sexual side effects. The best-selling antidepressant Prozac, for example, can reduce sexual desire and the ability to achieve orgasm in a substantial number of men and women, according to a variety of studies. Other conventional antidepressants similarly interfere with the enjoyment of life, which undoes many of their benefits.

If you are taking antidepressants to get through a bad time, such as the period following the death of a parent, you may be willing to tolerate these side effects. But if you are on antidepressants for a long time, perhaps for life, you are selling yourself short if you put up with side effects that make your days unpleasant.

SAM-e is a much better alternative. It works at least as well as conventional antidepressants but without any side effects except, in a few cases, mild stomach upset. As a natural substance, SAM-e is especially appropriate for older people who are often on many medications and who risk dangerous drug interactions when they take prescription antidepressants. It is also useful for those who feel nervous about flooding their bodies with chemicals. In fact, just about the only people who should *not* take SAM-e are those who suffer from manic-depression, in which moods can swing between intense lows (the depression) and extremely active highs (the manic phase). Like all other antidepressants, including the herbal sort, SAM-e can spark a manic episode.

SAM-e is also giving new hope to people afflicted with osteoarthritis, a condition in which joints wear down and become painful and stiff. Conventional treatments for this disease, which afflicts a majority of people over sixty-five, range from bad to worse. Bad are the daily doses of aspirin and nonsteroidal anti-inflammatory drugs (NSAIDs) like ibuprofen taken to relieve pain and reduce inflammation. These drugs not only cause significant damage to the stomach lining, often resulting in dangerous ulcers, but they also seem to destroy the cartilage that has already been ravaged by osteoarthritis.

Worse still are the cortisteroids. These synthetic hormones

dramatically reduce inflammation but are known to contribute to osteoporosis, a bone-thinning disease, and probably cause more damage to joint cartilage than NSAIDs do.

SAM-e reduces the pain and stiffness of arthritis without causing any significant side effects. There is also suggestive evidence that it may repair damaged cartilage. No wonder, then, that many arthritis sufferers consider SAM-e a miracle drug.

If the treatments for osteoarthritis are draconian, those for fibromyalgia verge on nonexistent. Fibromyalgia, which most often afflicts women in their thirties, is a variable condition that is usually diagnosed by a process of elimination combined with a standardized test for tender points on the body. Treatment includes low doses of antidepressants, which may not be highly effective.

Again, SAM-e comes to the rescue. European studies document that the natural supplement can ease the depression and muscle soreness associated with fibromyalgia.

SAM-e might also help heavy drinkers. Preliminary research suggests that supplementation by SAM-e can repair some of the liver damage caused by too much alcohol consumption or by viral illnesses like hepatitis. Other conditions that may respond to SAM-e include Parkinson's disease, heart disease, and Alzheimer's. The best-documented assistance, however, is for depression and arthritis.

WHAT TO EXPECT WITH SAM-e

When you take SAM-e you will feel more energetic in just a couple of days, whereas many conventional antidepressants can make you drowsy or foggy. With SAM-e, relief from depression occurs with almost lightning speed—within four to ten days—at least twice as fast as the swiftest conventional antidepressants and about six times faster than St. John's wort. In Europe, in fact, some clinicians prescribe SAM-e to elevate the mood of their patients while they are waiting for other antidepressants to kick in. Relief from osteoarthritis and fibromyalgia may take a bit longer, possibly two to four weeks.

A NOTE ON THE SCIENTIFIC METHOD

Throughout this book, you will find references to various scientific studies, most of which have been published in academic journals and have been peer-reviewed—meaning that other scientists have examined the material and made sure it is sound. In American journals, it is quite common for the first version of an academic article to be returned to the author for revisions based on the comments of the review panel, one reason, incidentally, that studies often seem to have taken place years before they are actually reported.

The best studies take into account the placebo effect. Because of mechanisms that are not well understood, a certain percentage of people will improve when given an inert drug simply because they believe they are being treated with a chemical that will help them. This placebo effect is exceptionally high with medication aimed at alleviating depression.

To isolate genuine effects, researchers conduct double-blind studies with control groups. "Double-blind" means that neither the subjects nor the researchers know who is getting an experimental drug and who is getting a placebo, a pharmacologically inert substance. These expectations would influence the results. A control group is a set of participants who take the placebo or get no treatment at all. Ideally, subjects are randomly assigned to either a control group or an experimental group to avoid any kind of consistent bias.

This scientific method, derived from the philosophical tenets of positivism, which considers perception by the senses the primary source of knowledge, has definite limitations. Sometimes, for instance, it has been difficult to come up with a placebo that resembles the experimental treatment closely enough so that study participants do not immediately know which they are getting. This has been a problem, for instance, with testing acupuncture, and is also difficult with drugs that have strong side effects, such as some antidepressants. Studies are also hampered when the dependent variable—the outcome—is difficult to quantify, as in the case of pain: people can rate pain on a scale but there is no way of knowing if one person's moderate pain is the same as another's. In addition, Tibetan and traditional Oriental medicine are hard to study because practitioners normally individualize medications for each patient. There is thus no one single experimental condition to dole out to a treatment group.

Controlled double-blind studies also tend to be suitable only for small questions (Is this new medicine better than an existing one?), not big ones. The Framingham Heart Study, which has followed over 5,000 people in a suburb of Boston since 1948, uncovered the importance of cholesterol in heart disease and has been one of the most influential medical studies in American history. Because of its breadth, however, it is not a controlled study. Similarly, much new nutrition information has been based on epidemiological studies—for instance, the finding of a correlation between red wine consumption and low heart disease rates—that are not very exacting.

There is an assumption among much of the American public, and even among medical professionals, that Western medicine is based solely on rigorous research. But the clinical studies used as a basis for drug approval in the United States are funded by pharmaceutical companies, who, at the very least, have a certain stake in seeing ambiguous data cast in a favorable light.[2] These tests, moreover, have been commonplace only for the last forty years; drugs already in common use did not undergo research. One scientist estimates that only 20 percent of children's treatments have good science behind them.[3]

And many drugs are prescribed for uses that have not received the approval of the Food and Drug Administration (FDA). Oral contraceptives, for instance, have been employed for decades to treat acne; it is only recently that one manufacturer obtained approval for this application. What's more, with the fast pace of new medical development, many techniques have never been tested. Researchers estimate that no strict proof of efficacy exists for half of all surgical and other medical procedures.

It is important to understand this, because alternative medicine is often attacked by U.S. doctors for being untested or unproven. While the charge may in fact be true on occasion, it is also hypocritical, since much of American medicine fits the same bill. In the case of SAM-e, the situation is mixed. An honest look at the research, judged by the scientific method, indicates that about half the studies are well done and about half are not—which still leaves a lot of evidence in SAM-e's favor.

HOW SAM-e CAME TO THE UNITED STATES

The passage of the 1994 Dietary Supplement Health and Education Act significantly increased public access to herbal and natural supplements. Steered through Congress by Senator Tom Harkin of Iowa, who was impressed by a friend's recovery after using alternative medicine, the law says that these products do not need to undergo the type of testing that is required for drug approval by the FDA. Manufacturers are now allowed to use labels with health claims that relate to the "structure-function" of the product—for example, the label of one brand of SAM-e says, "For joint support and mood." They are not able to state that they work against diseases—in other words, a producer of SAM-e cannot say it relieves arthritis and depression.

The advantage to consumers is that there is now a wide range of products available, and even the big vitamin brands like Centrum and One-A-Day have jumped on the herbal-supplement bandwagon. Between 1994 and 1998, the market for herbals soared 120 percent. This booming business—consumers spend an estimated $4 billion a year on alternative remedies—inspired Knoll SPa, the Italian company that makes SAM-e, and its German parent company BASF, to enter the United States in 1999 by giving licenses to three American firms. And that is how SAM-e, a prescription drug in fifteen countries, including Italy, Germany, Spain, Russia, and Argentina, became an over-the-counter supplement in the country with the world's tightest pharmaceutical controls.

BEING A SMART CONSUMER OF SAM-e

The big drawback to the Dietary Supplement Act is that there is no government oversight of the safety and efficacy of the supplements. It is of course not legal to sell a supplement that is dangerous or that is not what it claims to be, but the burden of proof is now on the FDA, which basically responds to complaints—that is, the FDA is more reactive than active.

You might think this doesn't matter. You may believe that supplement manufacturers are benign capitalists who can be trusted: the vitamin version of Ben & Jerry's. In reality, what looks like a benign world turns out to be filled with industrial espionage; "leakage," as one manufacturer put it (otherwise known as falling off the truck); and sheer chicanery. There is a lot of money here, and some of it is going into the pockets of latter-day snake oil salesmen. "You could make a bogus SAM-e product in your bathroom and easily sell it on the Internet," says Dr. Todd Henderson, vice president of Nutramax Laboratories, a highly regarded nutraceutical firm.

SAM-e is an interesting case, in that the German company BASF and its largest licensee, Pharmavite, have taken it upon themselves to protect the good name of the product, which can legally be manufactured by anyone. This would never happen with St. John's wort, which is not associated with any one company. Pharmavite has already spent over $100,000 in legal fees in an attempt to halt one vitamin chain store from distributing degraded, or chemically inactive, SAM-e.

Taking SAM-e can provide incredible benefits. But when you buy the supplement, you need to be an educated and skeptical consumer. *The SAM-e Handbook* will give you the information you need to use this exciting product wisely.

Chapter 2

WHAT MAKES SAM-e WORK?

Many people, when they first hear about SAM-e, respond with disbelief. How can it be? they wonder. How can one supplement possibly reduce both depression and arthritis, two illnesses that seem to have nothing in common? The answer is that SAM-e affects an extraordinarily broad range of internal functions, some of which relate to depression, some to arthritis, and some to other conditions.

Even with pharmaceutical (synthetic) drugs, wide-ranging effects are not uncommon. Aspirin, for instance, not only relieves the pain of headaches but also thins the blood, which is useful for some people at risk for strokes. Oral contraceptives prevent pregnancy but are also known to clear up acne in certain women. Thalidomide, the 1960s-era European sedative, caused heartbreaking birth defects in children whose mothers took it while pregnant, but it has recently shown promise at treating a disparate group of ailments, including leprosy (a bacterial disease), AIDS (a viral infection), and Crohn's disease (an inflammation of the intestines that causes diarrhea and is probably an autoimmune disorder). And the first modern antidepressant, iproniazid, was and still is used to treat tuberculosis; it was not used as an antidepressant for long because it produced unpleasant side effects.

SAM-e has a wide-reaching impact because it is a crucial

member of several important chemical relay teams. Found in cells throughout the body, but especially concentrated in the liver, S-adenosylmethionine is a molecule that combines methionine, an amino acid abundant in meat and dairy foods, with ATP (adenosine triphosphate), the body's main energy molecule. ATP fuels, among other things, muscle movement. Levels of SAM-e decline as we get older—children have seven times as much as adults—and are known to be low in some people who are depressed, have liver disease, and are afflicted with Alzheimer's disease.

The SAM-e power train is responsible for numerous actions:

- SAM-e facilitates the journey through the brain of neuro-transmitters (chemical messengers), which affect moods and energy levels.
- SAM-e keeps the membranes of cells fluid.
- SAM-e allows each cell, via DNA, to operate according to its precise building code.
- SAM-e helps reduce the inflammation that can cause pain.
- SAM-e prompts the release of natural painkillers.
- SAM-e promotes antioxidants that are crucial to the functioning of the joints and the liver.
- SAM-e aids the liver in detoxifying harmful substances.

THE MAGIC OF METHYLATION

SAM-e is an integral member of at least three chemical processes, the best known of which is called methylation.[1] In the process of methylation a molecule within the body "donates" a four-atom methyl group to another molecule. Both molecules become transformed by this procedure. This chemical relay happens about a billion times a second, and sparks anywhere from forty to one hundred vital biochemical processes. While SAM-e is by no means the only methyl donor in the body, it is by far the most active.

Methylation is crucial to our existence at the most basic level—DNA. DNA is like the software program of a cell; it tells the cell how to function and reproduce. Since each cell carries the entire genetic code of a human being inside it, there has to be a mechanism that turns some genes on and others off so that, for instance, a lung cell won't operate like a liver cell. An enzyme known as DNA methyltransferase transports methyl groups from SAM-e and donates them to DNA, which allows for genes to become activated or inactivated. Genes that receive a green light stimulate cell growth, restoration, and reproduction. Red lights can slow down tumor growth. One theory is that undermethylation—in effect, a failure to get the right green and red lights—is a contributing factor to cancer.

Boosting methylation has some fairly immediate effects. For example, the methylation of proteins (macromolecules composed of one or more chains of amino acids) has a profound impact on the brain. Within the brain, various nerve cells communicate by means of chemical messengers known as neurotransmitters. Three neurotransmitters—serotonin, norepinephrine, and dopamine—have been especially associated with depressed moods. Increasing methyl donors via SAM-e supplementation appears to improve the transmission of their chemical messages, resulting in a better mood. (This is explained in more detail in Chapters 3, 4, and 5.) SAM-e is also involved in the production of acetycholine, another neurotransmitter that helps people feel energetic and retain information.

Another beneficial process is the methylation of fatty substances called phospholipids that maintain the pliability of the walls of cells, including the nerve cells in the brain. When cell walls are flexible, more messages get through. SAM-e improves the permeability of these barriers, and some researchers attribute its quick improvement of depression—days instead of the weeks needed by prescription drugs—to this facilitation of neurochemical communication.

THE ANTIOXIDANT CONNECTION

After donating its methyl group SAM-e temporarily turns into an amino acid called homocysteine (more on this a little later). Some homocysteine, through a process known as transsulfuration (the release of sulfur groups), becomes transformed, with a boost from vitamin B_6, into the precursor of glutathione, a superpowerful antioxidant. Antioxidants neutralize free radicals, which are unstable and highly damaging oxygen-containing molecules that result from various assaults on the body, such as exposure to cigarette smoke, sunlight, dietary fats, and pesticides, as well as from several biochemical processes, like the breakdown of carbohydrates into a usable form of energy. In the liver, glutathione attaches to toxic substances, making them more water-soluble so that they can be eliminated from the body through urination. When glutathione is not available—generally the end result of a hepatitis infection or overconsumption of alcohol—the liver cannot adequately perform its detoxification function, and this creates a dangerous situation. Supplementing with SAM-e, therefore, provides huge benefits to the liver, at least in cases where the liver is damaged.

Glutathione toils as an antioxidant elsewhere in the body, too, helping to spare DNA from damage, protecting the lenses of the eyes, and quelling the inflammation that can cause pain in people with osteoarthritis.

Some people have suggested that you could get the benefits of glutathionine through direct supplementation, bypassing SAM-e. Although this antioxidant is indeed sold in health food stores, evidence suggests that it does not survive the stomach intact, so it has no therapeutic benefits. Transsulfuration brings another benefit to arthritis sufferers. By releasing the sulfur that was originally in SAM-e (that's what the capital S stands for), the process sets the stage for the production of glucosamine and chondroitin sulfate, which are crucial for building and maintaining the cartilage in joints. This is probably why SAM-e helps repair cartilage damaged through osteoarthritis.

There is an additional biochemical pathway through which SAM-e may benefit arthritis and fibromyalgia patients. SAM-e is involved in the creation of two polyamines, protein-like substances that affect cell function and release, as a by-product, chemicals that reduce inflammation and pain. Thus there is a second manner (a pathway called aminopropylation) in which SAM-e functions as a painkiller.

THE ISSUE OF HOMOCYSTEINE

We have already said that after SAM-e loses its methyl group, it becomes homocysteine—a name that may already sound familiar because of its association with heart disease. Think of homocysteine as the evil twin of SAM-e. Pileups of homocysteine in the bloodstream scar and harden the walls of arteries, setting in motion a process that can ultimately lead to heart disease and stroke. People with high levels of this substance in their blood are much more likely to experience heart attacks than others, according to a study of almost 15,000 physicians. For this reason, some medical researchers have questioned whether taking SAM-e supplements can increase the amount of this harmful substance in the body. However, "SAM-e does not increase homocysteine, according to both published and unpublished studies," says Dr. Teodoro Bottiglieri, research scientist at the Metabolic Disease Center at Baylor University in Dallas, and the country's leading researcher on the biochemistry of S-adenosylmethionine. "The body produces a lot more homocysteine than just what SAM-e causes. If anything, SAM-e stimulates the removal of homocysteine," he adds.

This is done partly through a process known as remethylation, in which some homocysteine gets recycled back into methionine. This activity requires the presence of two B vitamins—folic acid and B_{12}—which is why you are advised to take in the minimum daily values of these micronutrients. Shortfalls of folic acid and vitamin B frequently occur in people who are severely depressed or who have neurological disorders, and one explanation is that the shortages prevent adequate methylation in the body. However, supplementation with B vitamins alone rarely relieves depression. Nor will taking in supplements of the amino acid methionine, which, in large doses, can be toxic. The best way known to increase the amount of methyl donors in the body is to take supplements of SAM-e.

GETTING SAM-e INTO THE BLOODSTREAM

Although SAM-e is available in very small amounts in some foods, you can substantially increase your internal—endogenous—cache only by taking supplements, an exogenous source. It has been clearly documented that both injections and tablets of SAM-e raise the amount of the substance in your body.

The benefits of supplementation are easiest to understand for people who have liver disease caused by excess alcohol consumption or by a viral infection like hepatitis. These people often have a marked deficiency of SAM-e because their livers no longer produce the enzyme that turns the amino acid methionine into S-adenosylmethionine, which is crucial for the detoxification functions of the liver. Here, supplementation with SAM-e circumvents a flawed pathway and rectifies an obvious deficiency. This is similar to the way insulin injections allow diabetics to metabolize carbohydrates in the face of a shortfall of internally produced insulin.

Supplements can also work in a more subtle fashion. When your body is overloaded with SAM-e, it sparks some of the processes that SAM-e stimulates. "The purpose [of taking SAM-e] is to load the system with higher levels of raw material, in order to enhance a process that is already working....

[W]hen you load the system with SAM-e, you increase the supply of methyl donors. The body then uses the extra supply where it is most needed, as part of its innate self-regulating process," explain Colorado physician Sol Grazi and his coauthor in their book *SAMe: The European Arthritis and Depression Breakthrough* (Prima, 1999).

Injections (into veins, muscles, or a portion of the small intestine near the stomach) are the most efficient means of getting SAM-e into the body, and this was the form used in the earliest tests of the nutraceutical. A supplement only available as shots, of course, has limited usefulness, and in the 1980s a pill was developed by Knoll SPa in Italy. Since studies showed that SAM-e is broken down by stomach acids, this brand (which is now sold in the United States as Nature Made, GNC, and Nature's Bounty) came with an enteric coating—a coating, usually of some form of antacid like calcium carbonate, which does not dissolve in the stomach but which does disintegrate in the intestine. Once in the intestine, SAM-e can be distributed intact throughout the body. Studies also showed that SAM-e is better absorbed by the body when taken on an empty stomach.

SIDE EFFECTS: VIRTUALLY NONE

Because SAM-e is a substance already present in the body, it causes very little internal disruption. The most common complaint is minor gastrointestinal distress, such as an upset stomach, loose bowels, or gas. These symptoms usually go away within a week or so, but in the meantime you can reduce discomfort in the stomach by taking SAM-e before you eat a small snack. The supplement has also been known to cause headaches, although these generally disappear quickly.

SAM-e has an activating effect on most people, and this can lead to insomnia. For that reason, those who are new to the nutraceutical are advised to take the pill before evening. Similarly, people who suffer from severe anxiety may find that their nervousness becomes worse on SAM-e; a different treatment might be more suitable. Also, it is possible that, like many antidepressants, SAM-e can spark a panic attack, in which your heart races and you are almost paralyzed with fear. Finally, SAM-e, again like other antidepressants, is known to stimulate manic episodes—periods of intense activity accompanied by feelings of invulnerability—in people with a history of manic-depression (now known as bipolar disorder). Bipolar disorder is treated with a completely different set of drugs and nutraceuticals than garden-variety depression, and taking SAM-e is not an appropriate route.

HOW IS SAM-e MADE?

The production of S-adenosylmethionine is an intensely complicated procedure. For Nature Made, the brand of the California-based supplement company Pharmavite, the process begins in Switzerland near the Italian border. Here, under the auspices of its partner Knoll SPa, which manufactures prescription SAM-e for Europe, a special strain of yeast is cultured. The amino acid methionine is added into the yeast "soup," which causes the organism to produce a great deal of SAM-e. "When the yeast matures, we destroy it and extract the SAM-e," explains Marshall Fong, an executive with Pharmavite. "From forty to fifty parts of the yeast soup, we extract just one part of SAM-e," Fong says. This purification process is quite inefficient and costly.

This highly unstable substance is then shipped to a Knoll facility in Italy. Since SAM-e picks up water easily, it is manufactured into a stable compound in a climate-controlled environment (under 10 percent humidity), where the tablets are also given an enteric coating that protects against oxygen and digestion in the stomach. The pills are then sealed in double foil blisters to protect against moisture. These are shipped to a Pharmavite factory in southern California, where they are packaged.

Between the manufacturing process and the customs duties on a product made abroad, this brand of SAM-e does not come cheap. Nor do other formulations of SAM-e. Most reliable brands of SAM-e cost about a dollar for a 200 mg pill, which can really add up if you are taking two or four or eight a day. The unreliable brands—those without enteric coding, without protection from moisture, and sometimes even without measurable amounts of SAM-e—might be less expensive, but are not worth the bother. (See Chapter 12 for a closer look at the better brands.)

Pills may soon come down in price, at least for one brand. In mid-2000 Nature Made intends to move its tablet-manufacturing process from Italy to California, which should ultimately lower the cost to consumers by 30 percent. For people who shop at stores like Wal-Mart, the price per pill will

Tips on Taking SAM-e

1. Tell your doctor that you are taking SAM-e so that he or she can keep abreast of your progress and advise you of any additional avenues to pursue.

2. Do not take SAM-e, except under a doctor's close supervision, if you have any history of manic episodes, in which you are hyperactive and have feelings of grandiosity, or panic attacks, in which you are so afraid that your heart races uncontrollably, or if you are currently pregnant.

3. If you are taking any other drugs or supplements, either prescription or over-the-counter, notify your doctor to make sure that SAM-e will not interact in a negative way with any of these chemicals. (Negative interaction is unlikely except in the case of MAO inhibitors, a powerful prescription antidepressant.)

4. If your doctor has not heard of SAM-e—circumstance that is not hard to imagine—tell your pharmacist about your use of SAM-e. Pharmacists are usually very well informed about drug interactions. If a good pharmacist is not available, call one of the information lines set up by the various manufacturers or supplement outlets. (Phone numbers and Web sites appear in Chapter 12.)

5. Take one pill (or one set of pills) in the morning, a half hour before breakfast, and one in the afternoon. SAM-e is absorbed better on an empty stomach. Do not take the second pill after 7:00 P.M.—it might keep you awake. If

you have trouble remembering to take a pill in the afternoon, take two in the morning.

6. When you take your first pill of the day, also take a vitamin B complex tablet with 100 percent of the recommended daily allowance of the micronutrients.

7. If at any time you get so restless that you can't sit still, or if you start talking a mile a minute, stop taking SAM-e.

probably go down from about $1.00 to $.75, and for those who buy in bulk at warehouse stores like Costco, the price will drop even further, to about $.50 a pill.

For many this will still be more than the $5.00 or $10.00 co-payment they shell out under their insurance plans for prescription antidepressant or osteoarthritis drugs. And it is unlikely that SAM-e will become the (usually reimbursable) prescription drug it is in Europe. The reason is that the original formulation for manufacturing SAM-e (tosylate) is not patented, although Knoll's current, slightly more stable form (butane disultonate) is. Knoll would have to spend $300 to $350 million on testing to win FDA approval as a prescription drug over the course of about seven years, estimates Marshall Fong of Pharmavite. Then, once SAM-e was allowed behind pharmacist's counters, "every pharmaceutical company in the generic business would gear up to make it," he says. In other words, Knoll and other manufacturers have absolutely no financial incentive to turn SAM-e into a prescription drug.

Instead, Pharmavite is waging a modest campaign to get insurance companies to reimburse consumers for the cost of

SAM-e. And in a few cases, most of which involve people with liver damage where virtually no other treatment is available, the insurers have agreed.

The lack of insurance coverage does, however, carry a subtle advantage: there is no paper trail. Employers can and do gain access to their workers' records of prescription drugs, and they may discriminate against someone who uses antidepressants. Thus someone who wants to avoid creating proof of a disorder like depression may feel safer buying a mood brightener out of pocket.

And for people who have found relief with SAM-e without the irritating side effects of other medications, the price is not a serious obstacle. Says one woman who used SAM-e to overcome the debilitating aches of arthritis, "It seems funny to me that many people gripe about the cost. How can you compare the outlay of money with the cost of chronic pain? At least now I can be productive."

Chapter 3
THE BIRTH OF THE BLUES

We all have bad days, when we can't seem to get started, when nothing goes right, or when the future looks bleak. And we all suffer through unhappy periods after we've lost a loved one, endured a disappointment, or felt hurt. But sometimes bad days turn into bad weeks, bad months, and even bad years. And sometimes the sad days become so frequent that we can't remember living any other way. Sadness that won't quit is known as depression.

But depression is not just sadness. Some depressed people fall into a numb state in which they don't feel anything. For others the emotions come through in their bodies. They feel heavy and leaden, as if lifting their feet to walk is an incredible burden.

Depression alters daily life. Depressed people may have trouble sleeping and may lose interest in eating. They often withdraw from social activities and may isolate themselves from their families and friends. They think the future looks bleak. In severe cases they may think about suicide or even attempt it.

However it is manifested, depression is on the rise in industrialized societies. Younger people (from age eighteen to twenty-nine) have always had higher rates of this mood disorder than older persons, and the number of depressed younger people has increased in recent years, probably because the pressures on young people grow more intense with every generation. Those under thirty are much more likely than their baby boomer parents to have grown up in a broken home, which is often considered a risk for depression.

These days, an estimated 19 million Americans over age eighteen suffer from the chronic sadness of depression each year. Several million more feel a semipermanent malaise known as dysthemia. Both in the United States and abroad, women are almost twice as likely as men to experience depression. The elderly are not immune and may, in fact, be underdiagnosed, if they or their caregivers mistake symptoms of depression, like difficulty in remembering or concentrating, for those of aging. For most people, depression is a recurring ailment.

Many cases of depression clear up spontaneously—the average length of an untreated episode is nine months—but while the black moods continue they can cause a downward spiral. Depressed people are often short on energy, and they may lose their jobs because they can't fulfill their duties. Living with a depressed person is trying. Hence, many marriages become strained. Unemployment and divorce lead to further depression. Some depressed folks try to self-medicate their bad moods and become addicted to substances like alcohol and cocaine; an estimated 24 to 40 percent of people with mood disorders are substance abusers. New research suggests that depression can also harm a person's physical health.[1] It makes people more susceptible to heart disease and bone thinning, which is particularly dangerous for older women, who are already at risk for fractures.

Fortunately, depression is now a highly treatable ailment.

Unfortunately, many people are ashamed to admit they are depressed. Yet this disorder is no more embarrassing than, say, diabetes. Many accomplished people have struggled with depression, including humorist Art Buchwald, singer Alanis Morissette, Olympic diver Greg Louganis, writer William Styron, entertainer Dick Clark, astronaut Buzz Aldrin, newsman Mike Wallace, and musician Ray Charles. Depression is so prevalent that it's been called the common cold of emotional troubles. There is no reason to suffer needlessly.

A DISEASE OF BODY AND MIND

Western civilization encourages people to think of themselves as two different entities, a mind that has feelings and a body that experiences health or sickness. Yet medical science has repeatedly shown that emotional experiences, such as recurring stress, have a huge impact on a person's health by, for instance, increasing the risk of heart disease. Similarly, illnesses such as hypothyroidism (underactive thyroid) can cause tiredness and sadness. Physical and mental states can interact. Losing the ability to crochet because of arthritis in the hands, for instance, can also lead to sadness and even despair.

The split between the mind and body is the Berlin Wall of biology: an artificial separation destined to crumble. Nowhere is the silliness of the distinction more apparent than with depression. This apparent feeling-state often manifests itself in physical symptoms such as fatigue and loss of appetite. It is common for those who suffer solely from these kinds of symptoms to think they are not depressed while others around them believe they are.

Physiologically, people in the midst of depression are different from others. Depressed people often look and feel tired but it has recently been documented that their bloodstreams may be flooded with an activating chemical called cortisol, keeping them in a constant state of stress. The cortisol, or glucocorticoid, is the end result of activation of the hypothalamic-pituitary-adrenocortical (HPA) axis—a chemical journey from the hypothalamus, an area in the brain that regulates basic functions like sleep, appetite, and sexual arousal, to the pituitary gland, which controls some hormone production, to the cortex, or outer layer, of the adrenal gland, which secretes hormones like adrenaline, or epinephrine. This cascade of internal chemicals, which begins as a response to stressful events, starts in the brain's hypothalamus with the release of corticotropin-releasing hormone (CRH), a neuropeptide that sets off the next step along the pathway. The brains of depressed people show excess CRH. Further along in the HPA axis, the adrenal gland is enlarged in about one-third of people with depression.

Feeling depressed is also associated with altered levels of certain brain chemicals such as serotonin, norephedrine, and dopamine. Fiddling with these substances, as we shall see in the next chapter, has been the main thrust of conventional antidepressants. But it is unlikely that these brain chemicals are the primary biological spark to depression because their levels can change quickly in the brain without immediately affecting a patient's mood—that is, conventional antidepressants swiftly alter a person's brain chemicals but take several weeks to relieve depression. SAM-e, on the other hand, improves depression in a matter of days. Some newer research efforts on the biology of depression have shifted focus to the stress-related CRH, according to a recent report on mental health by the surgeon general.[2]

ONE WOMAN'S DESCENT INTO DEPRESSION

Even before her mentor died, Martha was not an extremely happy person. A single woman in her forties, Martha had a few close friends but often felt adrift. Although she is quite bright and personable, she moved from one underpaying job to another, always feeling she was not achieving her potential. Her last relationship with a man ended a few years back, and she saw no prospects in her future. Her family background was troubled, too. Her mother was distant and mentally troubled; her more loving father was killed in a car crash when she was in high school. The most stable part of her life was a volunteer organization she had joined. She became very close to its leader, a well-educated, charming, and welcoming man who became almost a father figure. When he died suddenly of a heart attack, Martha was paralyzed by grief. "I cried all day," she recalls. "I could barely get out of bed and often didn't make it to work." After a few weeks of despair, she sought help from a doctor.

WHY DO PEOPLE GET DEPRESSED?

Why do some people, like Martha, feel crushed by losses or setbacks while others bounce back quickly? Why do some people ruminate over their failures while others take them in stride? For reasons that are not clear, certain people seem to have been blessed with an innate resiliency that keeps them on an even keel. Many others, though, are thrown by the ups and downs of their lives. They have a vulnerability that sometimes sends them into a mild, moderate, or severe depression when they are under duress. (Of course, some duress, like being a prisoner of war, is so extreme that virtually anyone will have an intense reaction to it.)

Vulnerability to depression appears to be in part genetic. Identical twins, with identical genes, are twice as likely to show concordance, or agreement, in mood disorders as are fraternal twins with disparate genes (in other words, identical twins are more similar than fraternal twins), suggesting an important hereditary influence. One study of twins says that genetic factors explain about 36 to 44 percent of the variation in women, but little in men. Those who seem to have inherited vulnerability tend to experience more severe and more recurring forms of depression.

Clearly, however, environmental factors also contribute to depression. Research has shown that people at especially high risk for depression often experienced a difficult childhood that may have included the loss of a parent or a lack of parental warmth.[3] Being reared by a depressed parent or one who drinks too much or does drugs also increases a person's chances of becoming depressed.

Current crises can also spark episodes of depression. You may recall that Martha went into a serious tailspin after the death of her mentor. In a study of female twins, research by Dr. Ronald C. Kessler, a medical sociologist now at Harvard Medical School, found that the occurrence of any of several life events in a month tended to produce depression.[4] The toughest crises were the death of a close relative, assault, serious marital problems, and a divorce or breakup.

Day-to-day stress may be even harder on the psyche than one-shot crises. Such everyday stress—recurring fights with an adolescent child, constant negative comments by a spouse, a job with impossible deadlines, the strain of juggling work and family life—can take a big toll. People get worn out by problems that seem to have no solution. When stress is relentless, they may see no end, and succumb to depression. This is probably why single mothers are twice as likely to become depressed as married moms.

Women are highly susceptible to the quotidian kind of stress because their concerns cover a broader range of people than do those of men, and thus they experience "network" stressful events—that is, women suffer not only from their own problems but also from those of others, such as the marital woes of a sibling or the school-yard teasing of their child. A study by Dr. Kessler showed that married women tend to be in worse moods than their spouses because they experience more stressful events in the day, partly because of these network occurrences and also because they juggle more responsibilities.[5]

SYMPTOMS OF MAJOR DEPRESSION

When psychiatrists and psychologists say that someone is depressed, they most often mean that the person is suffering from major depression, a serious condition that should be treated right away. According to the American Psychiatric Association, you are in a major depression if you have five or more of the following symptoms every day or nearly every day for two weeks and if one of those symptoms is either number 1 or number 2:

1. You feel sad, blue, gloomy, down.
2. You do not enjoy things you normally find pleasant, such as your job, your children, sex, your hobbies, and other recreational activities.
3. Your appetite has increased or decreased or you have unintentionally lost a significant amount of weight.
4. You have trouble getting to sleep or staying asleep, or you sleep more than usual.
5. You are very agitated and restless, or you seem to move in slow motion.
6. You feel intensely tired or short on energy all day.
7. You feel guilty or worthless.
8. You have trouble concentrating, or you have trouble making even minor decisions such as what to eat for dinner.
9. You frequently think about suicide, you have formulated a suicide plan, or you have made a suicide attempt. *Important:* If this applies to you, run, don't walk, to a doctor, regardless of the rest of your responses. Medication, such as SAM-e and other antidepressants, can lift your mood and make you think of your future in a more positive way.

This list may sound arbitrary. If you have four symptoms instead of five, are you depressed? How about three? One study found that a yes answer to either number 1 or number 2 gave a good indication of whether or not a patient was depressed.[6] Other research has concluded that a significant number of people who appear distressed—over one-quarter—don't fit into a predetermined psychiatric category, which puts into question the usefulness of some standard definitions.[7]

Psychiatrists distinguish between depression and anxiety, a chronic state of apprehension and fearfulness, yet the two moods often go together.[8] In fact, patients who have symptoms of both disorders are more the rule than the exception. Physiologically, both states produce an elevation of the stress chemical CRH. And they both seem to have a long-term impact on the same site in the brain, the hippocampus (a seat of memory), which, along with the amygdala (a center of fear responses), activates the hypothalamic-pituitary-adrenocortical axis. Human imaging studies have found that the hippocampus is smaller in people who suffer from post–traumatic stress disorder and recurring depression.

Further, many medications intended for depression, like Prozac, have turned out to be effective treatments for anxiety-related problems like eating disorders, obsessive-compulsive behavior, and panic attacks. Thus it is no longer clear whether the differentiation of depression and anxiety makes sense. The bottom line is that if you feel distressed, you should seek a solution—even if no one knows how to categorize your problem.

OTHER KINDS OF DEPRESSION

Atypical depression is different from typical depression in that the sufferers are able to experience pleasure. When depressed, they sleep and eat more. And even when they are not in the midst of a depressive episode, they have an acute sensitivity to social rejection that can interfere with their ability to sustain relationships and thrive in a career.

A more unusual form of depression is seasonal affective disorder (SAD), which occurs only during the fall and winter. People suffering from SAD crave carbohydrates and often gain weight; they sleep longer than normal and show a pronounced decline in energy. Scientists believe that this ailment is brought on by the reduced light levels in the colder seasons; the low light may increase the production of a sleep-inducing hormone known as melatonin and may also affect the availability of the neurotransmitters serotonin and norepinephrine, which are related to mood. The incidence of SAD is higher in northern areas where days are shortest in the winter. Thus only 1.4 percent of people in Florida suffer from seasonal affective disorder, but 9.7 percent of New Hampshire residents do, according to the National Institute of Mental Health. For people suffering from SAD, the treatment of choice is exposure to artificial light that mimics bright sunlight for from fifteen minutes to two hours a day.

A more serious problem is postpartum depression, which is more severe than the mild blues that often follow childbirth. A downbeat mood, at least partly caused by rapidly declining hormone levels, is a major concern for both mother and child if it lasts for more than a couple of days. Sufferers should seek treatment immediately.

Bipolar disorder, which used to be known as manic-depression, is another ailment that should be attended to swiftly. About 1.7 percent of the adult population suffers from the condition. Manic-depressives experience typical depressive symptoms but also go through manic periods in which they are hyperactive and feel on top of the world. Less commonly, they may be paranoid. Sometimes their mood switches are sudden and dramatic, but most frequently the changes are slow and subtle. Mania can be quite pleasant for the person in its midst, though not for relatives and co-workers, and thus the sufferer may not be motivated to end it.

While major depression is much more common among women, manic-depression appears to be equally distributed between the sexes. It also has a strong inherited element. The risk of bipolar depression is six to eight times greater among people with a first-degree relative (parent, sibling) who has the disorder; for ordinary depression, that figure is two to four. These numbers, of course, also reflect some environmental influences since relatives grow up in the same house.

The distinctive hypomanic episodes, by definition, last at least four days and involve three or more of these symptoms:

1. Hypomanic people have an inflated sense of self-worth or a grandiose self-image.
2. They need less sleep than usual and may feel rested after three hours in bed instead of the usual eight.
3. They are more talkative than usual and have trouble stopping themselves from talking.
4. Their thoughts are racing, and they keep shifting from one topic to another during conversation.
5. They are very easily distracted, even by minor things like the sound of heat going on in an apartment.
6. They overdo work, school, and social or sexual activities.

7. They engage in enjoyable activities, such as shopping beyond their means or having illicit sexual relationships, without regard for the risks.

If you have any of the symptoms of mania, don't try to treat your illness on your own. Manic-depression calls for a different set of drugs than depression: lithium, for instance, is very effective at putting bipolar depression under control. It is equally important to be aware that even the mildest antidepressants, including the herb St. John's wort and SAM-e, can set off a manic episode. If you have even the slightest reason to suspect bipolar depression, or if there is a history of the condition in your family, consult a physician before using any medication.

ANGST WITHOUT END

A much milder form of depression called dysthymia often goes untreated. For over 7 million Americans—perhaps 3 to 6 percent of the population on any given day—life is like a box of chocolates that someone else got to first: it's empty. Sufferers, who appear to have been born with dysthymia almost always see the glass as half empty. They complain of a lack of energy and often seem stuck in low gear. Their gloomy approach to life makes it hard for them to maintain relationships and thrive at work, though some are highly successful despite their emotional burdens. In other words, unlike people in the midst of a major depression, they are able to function in their day-to-day life. Unfortunately, though, dysthymics are highly susceptible to intermittent episodes of major depression, during which they are said to suffer from "double depression."

Dysthymia (sometimes translated as "ill-humored") used to be considered a fluke of temperament and hence not alterable by drugs, but it has recently been quite successfully treated with antidepressants like SAM-e and Prozac. It is, however, often missed by doctors.[9]

You may be diagnosed with dysthymia if you have been blue most days in the last two or more years and have experienced, while depressed, two or more of these symptoms:

1. You are eating more or less than usual.
2. You have trouble sleeping or you sleep more than usual.
3. You feel fatigued and low on energy.
4. You have a poor image of yourself.
5. You have trouble concentrating or making decisions.
6. You feel devoid of hope.

GETTING EXPERT FEEDBACK

Do you recognize yourself in any of the descriptions in this chapter? If you have any symptoms of depression, your first stop should be your doctor's office. The doctor can screen you for depression and rule out physical causes for your impaired moods, including diseases such as stroke, hypothyroidism, and pancreatic cancer, and medications like oral contraceptives and high blood pressure drugs. Just remember that primary care doctors like family physicians and internists do not specialize in mood disorders and may err on the cautious side. If you feel that something is wrong with your mood, you are probably right.

It is also important to realize that scientific opinion is moving in the direction of calling depression a recurring or chronic disease.[10] Although it is possible to experience a depressive occurrence just once in your lifetime, according to research, 80 percent of people will have at least one more episode. And about 12 percent suffer from major depression continuously. This means that if you think you have a problem, you should invest in a happier future by acting to improve your mood now. However, as we shall see in the next chapter, the antidepressants prescribed by doctors are often not the best solution.

Chapter 4

WHAT'S WRONG WITH CONVENTIONAL ANTIDEPRESSANTS?

For centuries, millions of people suffered from depression with little hope of relief. Until the mid-1950s in America, depression was considered solely a psychological problem and hence curable only by psychoanalysis or other psychotherapies, which were usually available to a wealthy few and even then were often ineffective. In the most severe cases, doctors sometimes relied on electroconvulsive shock, which stimulates brain seizures and which gained, rightly or wrongly, a reputation as a draconian treatment.

Then tuberculosis researchers testing iproniazid discovered that their depressed patients were becoming happier. The drug was a runaway success as an antidepressant in the late 1950s, but it fell quickly out of favor for this use after a small number of patients developed jaundice as a side effect. Iproniazid, which is still used against TB, proved that a huge market existed for effective antidepressants. Soon an entirely different kind of antidepressant, Tofranil (imipramine) was developed, and a new era began. The advent of these drugs, along with antipsychotic medications like Thorazine (chlorpromazine), was as important to sufferers of mental illness as was the development of antibiotics to people with infectious diseases. For millions of people, these drugs made life worth living. Most conventional antidepressants, regardless of their mode of action, relieve at least 50 percent of the symptoms for about 70 percent of people suffering from depression.

Yet the side effects of such antidepressants have been so intense that many who could benefit from medication have decided to suffer instead. Some people prefer the despair of depression to feeling foggy, being impotent, getting restless, lying awake at night, and risking a stroke—to name only a few of the possible side effects.

The most publicized wave of antidepressants—the Prozac generation—cut down on the side effects, and because of that reduction a whole new group of people, including those suffering from mild depression, began seeing medication as a tenable possibility. By one account, over 65 million prescriptions for antidepressants were filled in the United States in 1997. Three antidepressants, including Prozac, are among the top fifteen best-selling drugs in America.

But many users of the newer antidepressants, too, have been disappointed by side effects like the dampening of sexual interest. Side effects can be especially harmful to elderly people who are not as robust as younger people and who are probably taking a whole array of medications. And these newer antidepressants still do not offer fast relief. They may take up to three weeks to really kick in.

A recent on-line survey by the National Depressive and Manic-Depressive Association found an astonishing amount of discontent with antidepressants.[1] Of 1,400 patients who had used them within the past five years, some 81 percent said that their depression continued to impair their social life "moderately" or "extremely" while they were taking the pills.

Depression continued to negatively affect the family lives of 79 percent of the respondents, and interfered with work performance of 72 percent.

For many of those polled, the drugs not only failed to improve an energy problem but may have made it worse. Some 60 percent said that their medication caused drowsiness, 40 percent reported no improvement in fatigue and loss of energy, and 17 percent stopped taking medication because of side effects like insomnia and sexual dysfunction.

The experiences of these respondents are echoed by others who have taken antidepressants. "I'd eat ground glass before I'd take psychoactive drugs," says one woman who tossed out her meds.

For many people, SAM-e is a marked improvement over conventional antidepressants. It has no serious side effects and generally reaches full force in a week. In contrast, some antidepressants, especially the older ones developed two generations ago, are downright dangerous.

DAVE'S TRIP TO THE EMERGENCY ROOM

Dave was a golden boy. Handsome, athletic, and smart, he breezed through his Ivy League college and easily garnered a high-paying job at a white-shoe bank in a big northeastern city. He quickly settled into the lifestyle everyone predicted he would always have—a sweet and beautiful girlfriend, a membership at the right country club, a tasteful apartment. As the obedient son of a military officer, he had never questioned his parents' expectations. But slowly his life unraveled. After two years behind a desk, he found his job tedious and meaningless, and the salary was no compensation for how he spent fifty-odd hours a week. His girlfriend, whom he dearly loved, had no sympathy for his unease. Dave's performance fell off. Finally his supervisors offered him a deal. They would give him a year's salary if he would quietly leave.

That sounded like nirvana to Dave; he would finally have time to figure out what he really wanted to do with his life. But after a few weeks of organizing his week around grocery store sales, he started to slip into a deep funk. When his frustrated girlfriend ended their relationship, his mood only got worse. His parents noticed how flat he sounded and insisted he visit a psychiatrist. The psychiatrist prescribed Nardil (phenelzine), a potent MAO inhibitor–type antidepressant. Dave had always been careful about how he ate, so the dietary restrictions necessitated by the drug regimen did not feel burdensome.

For six months Dave hung out in his neighborhood, not exactly depressed but rather aimless. He had several girlfriends, none too serious, and all willing to accept the impotence he developed after starting the Nardil. One night at a local bar he tossed back a Czech beer and quickly went into a hypertensive crisis—his blood pressure skyrocketed, putting him at risk for a stroke. His date rushed him to an emergency room and made such a racket that he was tended to quickly. "I thought I was going to die," he recalls of that night. "This sounds like a cliché, but when I realized that I would be all right I decided that I had better do something with my life before my time ran out."

Dave went off the Nardil for three weeks—during which time his erectile dysfunction ceased—then resumed the medication. Energized by his brush with death, he applied to forestry schools in the West. "I wanted to be in the Big Sky country, away from the status-conscious cities. I wanted to spend my days outside, helping people and helping the environment," he says. Dave's parents surprised him by supporting his decision. By the time he left for Montana, he'd tapered off the antidepressants. "The drugs saved me by almost killing me," he says. This, of course, is not how antidepressants are supposed to help people.

HOW MOST ANTIDEPRESSANTS WORK

According to the theory behind current antidepressants, depression is rooted in the nerve cells, or neurons, of the brain. The 10 billion or so neurons in the brain are connected in a complicated manner. Separated by incredibly small spaces known as synapses, they come close to each other but do not touch. When a nerve cell is stimulated either electrically or chemically, the tip of that cell releases a substance known as a neurotransmitter, which crosses the gap and stimulates the next nerve cell, which repeats the process through an entire pathway. Neurotransmitters cannot make these leaps, however, unless the next nerve cell has the appropriate receptor and that receptor is activated, or turned on. Once a neurotransmitter has finished its task, it returns to its original cell. The original cell reabsorbs neurotransmitters by means of receptors known as uptake pumps. If the uptake pumps are out of commission, the neurotransmitters collect in the synapse, leaving more of them around to convey messages.

Of perhaps two hundred neurotransmitters, there are three

monoamines that have been most closely identified with shifts in moods. They are serotonin, norepinephrine, and dopamine. Serotonin shot to fame in the 1980s with the runaway success of a diet book called *The Carbohydrate Craver's Diet* (Ballantine, 1983), by Dr. Judith J. Wurtman, a nutrition researcher with the Massachusetts Institute of Technology. Dr. Wurtman claimed that eating carbohydrates would boost the level of serotonin, which would not only reduce carbohydrate cravings but would also calm people down. Although the diet ceased to be trendy, the association between serotonin and relaxation remains in the public's mind. Indeed, one of serotonin's functions in the body is to inhibit the stress pathway that causes, among other things, feelings of panic.

In contrast, the other two neurotransmitters, norepinephrine and dopamine, which are close cousins of adrenaline, are, to oversimplify a complicated situation, more associated with energizing moods. Dopamine is also connected to the pleasurable experiences (for some) that come from many illicit drugs. Addictive drugs like cocaine and heroin are known to raise dopamine among users.

Research has shown that the amount of these three neurotransmitters is low in the spinal fluid around the brains of depressed people. It is believed that antidepressants improve moods by altering, in susceptible people, the availability of these brain chemicals through a variety of circuitous means. They will not significantly lift the mood of someone who is not depressed—you can't get high on Prozac—and they are not known to create a dependence the way addictive drugs do.

This theory of depression—the so-called monoamine

hypothesis—has significant flaws, chief among them being the several-weeks-long lag in time between a change in monoamine neurotransmitter levels in the body and a shift in mood. Another flaw is that several other neurotransmitters are changed during depressive episodes. According to *Mental Health: A Report of the U.S. Surgeon* (1999), "Despite the problems with the hypothesis that monoamine depletion is the *primary* cause of depression, monoamine impairment is certainly one of the manifestations, or correlates, of depression. Therefore the monoamine hypothesis remains important for treatment purposes."

THE ANTIDEPRESSANT EXPERIENCE

Maybe you will walk out of a doctor's office with a prescription for an antidepressant that will boost your mood adequately in three weeks with no significant side effects and that will be the end of it. If so, you'll be lucky.

Odds are, however, that your doctor will need to tinker with your drugs. Because of quirks in individual biochemistry, one antidepressant may not relieve depression but another will. Or a drug that helps your depression may have side effects that make your life miserable. New drugs, such as tranquilizers or sleeping pills or Viagra (for impotence), may get added into your regimen. Or your doctor will keep changing the dose of the antidepressant you are taking to reduce the side effects.

Prescription antidepressants can and do help people, but they have many drawbacks. People who spend their lives having medications adjusted report that they feel like walking science experiments. This is the way one woman describes a highly medicated phase in which she unpredictably vacillated from feeling fine to being too calm to being revved up: "I was feeling like a Marx Brother at a drug circus."

Let's look at some of your options.

MAOIs: EFFECTIVE BUT SCARY

Monoamine oxidase inhibitors are among the oldest prescription antidepressants. They stop neurons from breaking down their excess neurotransmitters, resulting in an increased level of the chemicals inside the nerve cell. Presumably this higher level of serotonin, norepinephrine, or dopamine accounts for the drug's mood-elevating effects. These drugs work well at relieving depression. However, because of their serious side effects—such as the hypertensive crisis that prompted Dave's trip to the emergency room—they are often perceived as a medication of last resort.

MAOIs act by disabling an enzyme called monoamine oxidase. This enzyme, which is present in the liver and intestine as well as in brain cells, is also necessary for breaking down the amino acid tyramine, which is found in large amounts in certain aged cheeses and other foods. If you are taking an MAOI such as Nardil (phenelzine), Marplan (isocarboxazid), or Parnate (tranylcypromine), and you eat a tyramine-rich food, a cascade of unpleasant events ensues. The tyramine fails to be dismantled and instead enters your bloodstream intact, then moves into the body's cells, causing the release of norepinephrine, which can make blood pressure rise quickly. Result? Flushed skin, a severe headache in the back of the head, vomiting, and—the worst-case scenario—a life-threatening stroke.

Anyone on an MAOI must follow a restricted diet. While it is possible to consume small amounts of foods with moderate tyramine levels (such as bottled or canned beer and white or red wines, except for Chianti), the list of verboten foods is long: aged cheese, anchovies, broad beans, liver, overripe bananas, pickled meats, soy sauce, tap beer, and others. If you stop taking MAOIs you must wait at least two weeks to resume eating these foods, since the drug remains in your system.

You must also avoid many drugs while you are taking MAOIs, particularly those with stimulant qualities such as appetite suppressants, decongestants, and others used for asthma, coughs, and allergies, as well as the illicit drugs cocaine and methamphetamine. Taking additional antidepressants in conjunction with MAOIs can cause an overproduction of serotonin, which can lead to rapid heartbeat, high blood pressure, hyperactivity, and seizures.

Even people who steer clear of these foods and drugs can experience other side effects, chief among them insomnia, impotence, low blood pressure on standing (which causes faintness), dizziness, sedation, constipation, and rapid heartbeat. Although MAOIs are said to be especially effective for people with atypical depression, which is characterized by overeating, oversleeping, and oversensitivity to rejection, you can see why MAOIs are not on the top of anyone's list of antidepressants.

TRICYCLICS: PESKY SIDE EFFECTS

Available since the Truman years, tricyclic antidepressants, sometimes known as TCAs, were until recently the first drugs a doctor would prescribe for someone who was depressed.

Frequently used TCAs are Elavil (amytriptyline), Tofranil (imipramine), Norpramin (desipramine), Pamelor (nortriptyline), and Doxepin (sinequan). The drugs are believed to work by blocking the reuptake of the neurotransmitters serotonin and norepinephrine, in effect making them more plentiful in the brain. Chemically similar to antihistamines (used in allergy and cold remedies), some tricyclics have a stronger impact on serotonin while others seem to affect norepinephrine more, but all of these drugs have a broad-based pharmacological action that is blamed for their high rate of side effects.

Elavil, for instance, is quite sedating, which might be helpful for someone who can't sit still but would make most depressed people groggy and foggy. Tofranil interferes with a neurotransmitter (acetylcholine) that blocks the body's fight-or-flight reaction, thus causing stress responses such as fast heartbeat, perspiration, dry mouth, and constipation. Other common problems with tricyclics include blurry vision, weight gain (as much as 30 pounds), urinary problems, memory loss (in the elderly), and some unpleasant sexual difficulties (decreased sexual desire, impotence, trouble reaching orgasm, and, for women, decreased vaginal lubrication). It is possible to treat some of the side effects with additional drugs, but the piling on of medication makes many people uncomfortable. And patients are advised to avoid alcohol, sedatives, and oral contraceptives.

The tricyclics reduce depression in about 60 to 70 percent of patients, which is as good as current antidepressants get, and Tofranil is often the drug against which newer medications are compared in clinical studies. But because of the very real and unpleasant side effects of TCAs, many people discontinue their use. In other cases, family doctors will lower the dosages to reduce the side effects. Unfortunately, this often reduces the main effects so that people do not receive the mood-changing benefits they want.

With the advent of Prozac and similar drugs, tricyclics have become much less popular. Because they are relatively cheap, however, some managed care insurance companies have insisted that they be tried first before the much more expensive Prozac is covered.

PROZAC: A MIRACLE DRUG?

Selective serotonin reuptake inhibitors (SSRIs) such as Prozac (fluxetine), Zoloft (sertaline), and Paxil (paroxetine hydrochloride) have become among the best-known drugs in America. Prozac now accounts for about 44 percent of the $3 billion conventional antidepressant market, and Zoloft makes up about one-third. As the class name suggests, these drugs directly target serotonin, making it more available, and acting like a smart bomb compared to the unfocused blast of the tricyclics. New evidence from the University of California at San Francisco suggests that Prozac, Zoloft, and Paxil may also affect mood by increasing the synthesis of a steroid found in the brain that operates with a completely different neurotransmitter, called GABA (for gamma-aminobutyric acid). The antianxiety drug Valium works by stimulating this pathway; alcohol also affects it. GABA, like serotonin, inhibits a stress pathway. The older tricyclics tested had no effect on GABA.

The SSRIs have become immensely popular because they produce fewer side effects than the tricyclics, presumably because of the narrower focus of their activity. Many people who previously were not treated for moderate or mild depression are now willing to try medication because the side effects are tolerable. Yet side effects still afflict a substantial number of those who take these drugs. One study of Prozac cited adverse reactions in the following percentage of subjects: nausea (21%), headaches (20%), nervousness (15%), insomnia (14%), drowsiness (12%), diarrhea (12%), and dry mouth (10%). Other common complaints include weight gain or loss, sexual dysfunction (similar to that for the tricyclics), anxiety, dizziness, and skin rashes.

Here's how one woman describes her experience with Zoloft, which was prescribed for depression that seemed to stem from the hormonal churning of menopause: "The Zoloft relieved the depression but really zonked me out. I was sleepy all the time and emotionally pretty detached at any dose that worked to relieve depression. I went off of it because I got nothing done and was beginning to feel that it was only a numb veneer over my despair."

ST. JOHN'S WORT: HERBAL ISN'T ALWAYS BETTER

Because of dissatisfaction with conventional antidepressants, many Americans in recent years have turned to an herbal remedy widely used in Europe, particularly in Germany. St. John's wort, a plant that grows wild in the Northern Hemisphere, has become one of the best-selling supplements in vitamin stores and natural pharmacies. Like other herbal treatments, St. John's wort includes a number of chemicals—an estimated fifty in all—and scientists do not know which among them is responsible for the different effects of the herb. People who use naturopathic medicine applaud the diffuse nature of herbals, partly because it means that the drug will most likely be gentle in its actions. And it is true that St. John's wort, like SAM-e, has few side effects—mild stomach or intestinal distress, fatigue, confusion, risk of sunburn, and, most seriously, increased risk of cataracts. Some people get headaches because they clench their jaws.

Those who use herbal medications have a saying: "A whole plant to treat a whole person." For these people, the inchoate nature of herbals is an advantage. Western scientists, though, often get nervous when the pharmaceutically active agent in a medicine is not isolated.

St. John's wort is believed to help depression, at least in part, by improving the level of serotonin in the brain, although it may also affect the other neurotransmitters and could possibly be part of the GABA pathway.

The main problem with St. John's wort is that it has limited usefulness. St. John's wort is used mainly to relieve mild depression, not the stronger depression handled by SAM-e and other drugs. And it is a somewhat sedating drug, so it is not useful for the many depressed people who feel low on energy. It may also interact negatively with other drugs, reducing their effectiveness. In February 2000 the FDA sent out an advisory to American physicians cautioning them that St. John's wort can interfere with the functioning of oral contraceptives as well as drugs used to treat heart disease, depression, seizures, AIDS, and certain cancers.

There is additionally a problem in generalizing from studies conducted in Europe, where herbal drug quality control is high, to the United States, where loopholes in the drug laws allow supplements to reach the shelves without inspection by the Food and Drug Administration. For this reason, you often do not know what you are getting when you buy the herbal product off the shelf. Also, you need to know that the chemical the best brands are now standardized for—hypericin—may not be the chemical responsible for the antidepressant effects. According to current thinking, that important ingredient is likely a chemical called hyperforin.[2]

In addition, Americans are used to swallowing pills, and this is the most easily available form of the herbal, but it has usually been tested in Europe as a liquid extract. Dr. Jonathon Zeuss, an Arizona physician and author of *The Natural Prozac Program: How to Use St. John's Wort, the Antidepressant Herb* (Three Rivers Press, 1997), recommends taking this herb as an extract because this medium preserves the active ingredients best.

Finally, like all antidepressants except SAM-e, St. John's wort takes an extremely long time to act—up to six weeks, even longer than the tricyclics. "It might have helped if I had waited the full twelve weeks," admits one woman, who gave up after ten, "but who is going to sit around feeling bad for that long?"

A QUESTION OF TIMING

One of the biggest problems with antidepressants is that they tend to improve the somatic symptoms of depression, such as low energy, quicker than they relieve the mood disorders. Thus with conventional drugs people can and do get the energy to kill themselves before the mood-elevating effects of the pharmaceuticals kick in. This is particularly a problem with antidepressants (such as the MAO inhibitors and many of the tricyclics) that are lethal in an overdose.

SAM-e is different. Working through completely different mechanisms than either St. John's wort or the conventional antidepressants, it generally takes effect within one week. For some people, changes may happen sooner. In fact, physicians in Europe may prescribe SAM-e in combination with an antidepressant drug so that the patient will get mood-elevating effects almost right away. The fast-acting quality of SAM-e is one of its strongest benefits. You'll hear more about this in the next chapter.

Chapter 5

BEATING DEPRESSION WITH SAM-e

Hundreds of thousands of Americans suffering from mild, moderate, and severe depression have turned to SAM-e since it became available in the United States in March of 1999. Grateful users report that they are able to get up in the morning and go to work each day. Women have the energy to leave abusive relationships. Some people are motivated to go to school and change fields. Others begin to enjoy their children rather than viewing them as one more stress in their lives.

A substance that is already found in the body, SAM-e has enormous advantages over conventional prescription antidepressants. Unlike the more toxic prescription drugs, SAM-e produces almost no side effects, certainly none of the problems that interfere with maintaining a happy life such as the inability to enjoy sex. Again, unlike prescription drugs, the mood-elevating benefits of SAM-e are experienced quickly, sometimes within days rather than the weeks it takes other drugs to work. Also, unlike some prescription drugs, SAM-e is not fatal if taken in an overdose, an important consideration for people who are severely depressed and potentially suicidal. And unlike some herbal and prescription antidepressants, SAM-e is an energizer. It lifts people out of their lethargy and helps them find pleasure in their lives.

An essential member of numerous chemical relay teams, SAM-e relieves depression through multiple pathways. As with conventional antidepressants, but probably through different mechanisms, SAM-e appears to enhance the actions of three neurotransmitters (monoamines) connected to moods—serotonin, norepinephrine, and especially dopamine. SAM-e is known to methylate fats called phospholipids that are the main component of cell membranes. By making brain cells more permeable, it probably assists the journey of neurotransmitters through the brain. SAM-e is also believed to improve the ability of neurotransmitters to bind to the cells that are their destinations. SAM-e affects other brain chemicals as well, though the exact details are not well understood. "It clearly works differently than other antidepressants," says Dr. Bruce Kagan, a professor of psychiatry at the University of California, Los Angeles, School of Medicine.

Whatever the precise mechanisms, it is obvious that SAM-e works fast against depression—far faster than the prescription antidepressants and the herb St. John's wort.

THE SCIENTIFIC EVIDENCE FOR
SAM-e'S EFFECTIVENESS

SAM-e relieves depression in about 60 to 70 percent of people who take it, according to a significant body of scientific research. For the last twenty-five years, millions of people have used SAM-e successfully in Europe, particularly in Italy, to combat depression—with virtually no serious side effects reported. Since the 1970s, some forty clinical studies on

SAM-e and depression have appeared in the scientific litera-ture, involving around 1,400 patients—low, perhaps, by the standards of the U.S. Food and Drug Administration, but impressive when combined with the positive experiences of real people who have taken the supplement. "I believe that S-adenosylmethionine has been as well tested as many other drugs on the U.S. market," says Dr. Lewis Opler, a psychiatrist with a Ph.D. in pharmacology who is an adjunct professor at Columbia University's College of Physicians and Surgeons.

Generally, research shows SAM-e to work better than place-bos and to be as effective as tricyclic antidepressants but faster-acting and with far fewer side effects. TCAs, as noted earlier, can cause fogginess and dry mouth, and often take three to four weeks or more to work. In contrast, SAM-e's main side effect is a minor stomachache, and people usually feel better within four to seven days. To date, no published study has compared SAM-e with the newer antidepressants like Prozac, which tend to have an effectiveness similar to the tricyclics with milder, though still potent, side effects.

A 1994 meta-analysis, which combined several small stud-ies to increase statistical power, found important evidence of SAM-e's effectiveness.[1] The admittedly flawed research—it mixed studies that used oral SAM-e with those in which the substance was injected—concluded that SAM-e has a greater impact on depression than placebos and an effect similar to that of TCAs. An interesting California study published the same year discovered that people who showed a 50 percent improve-ment in depression scores also displayed an increase in SAM-e levels in the blood, regardless of whether they had taken a tricyclic antidepressant or SAM-e.[2] The authors speculated that conventional antidepressants may work, in part, by elevating levels of SAM-e in the body.

Two very small studies also suggest that SAM-e is appropriate for people with severe or intractable depression.[3] One double-blind study, done at the West Los Angeles Veterans Administration Center in California, found that oral doses of SAM-e effectively altered the moods of patients hospitalized for depression, who are likely to be highly disabled by their disorder. In an open study among outpatients at Massachusetts General Hospital, two out of nine treatment-resistant subjects experienced full relief. Although this percentage sounds small, and certainly the number of subjects is minuscule, it does suggest that some people who fail on conventional antidepressants—an estimated 10 to 20 percent of patients—may respond to SAM-e.

A definitive study on SAM-e is currently being conducted by Pharmavite, the California-based corporation that distributes the nutraceutical under license from a European firm. With an anticipated end date in late 2001, the multicenter $4 million trial will test the efficacy of SAM-e alone, SAM-e in combination with an SSRI antidepressant, an SSRI alone, and a placebo, in relieving major depression for about 360 subjects over the course of sixteen weeks. "It is one of the largest studies ever on a dietary supplement," says Marshall Fong of Pharmavite.

WHO SHOULD TAKE SAM-e

Anyone who is depressed stands a good chance of feeling better with SAM-e, but some people are especially likely to reap the benefits from this natural supplement:

- *People with low energy* benefit from the activating properties of SAM-e.
- *People who need immediate relief* are happy to see their moods improve in just a few days. Quick benefits can result from using SAM-e under a doctor's supervision, while waiting for a prescription antidepressant to kick in.
- *The elderly,* who often take many medications that may interact with prescription antidepressants, may feel safer taking a supplement with few side effects.
- *People with both depression and arthritis*—in other words, a large number of people over fifty—can relieve two ailments with one treatment.
- *People who haven't succeeded with any other drug* have another option with SAM-e. About 20 percent of people with depression do not respond adequately to the first two antidepressants they try, and possibly 10 percent don't respond to anything.
- *People who take antidepressants for the long term* can remain on SAM-e indefinitely because of the lack of side effects.
- *People who enjoy having a drink or two* will appreciate the fact that SAM-e does not appear to interact with alcohol, unlike many other antidepressants. Of course, exces-

sive drinking can lead to depression, so stick to only a few a day.

- *People who also have liver disease* can rest assured that SAM-e does not hurt the liver, and probably helps it.
- *People who want natural medicine* feel more comfortable with a substance that is already found in the human body.

WHO SHOULD NOT TAKE SAM-e

SAM-e is suitable for most people, but there are exceptions. If you have any history of the hyperactive episodes known as mania, or if anyone in your family has a history of manic-depression, which is highly inheritable, then you should not take the supplement except under the close supervision of a physician. In a handful of documented cases, SAM-e seems to have pushed depressed people into a manic state. Similarly, if you are susceptible to panic attacks—in which your heart beats quickly and you are almost paralyzed with fear—SAM-e, like other antidepressants, can spark an incident. Do not take the supplement without first consulting your doctor.

Another difficult situation can occur with people who are taking MAO inhibitors, which, as you recall from the last chapter, can trigger a hypertensive crisis. These drugs should never be combined with any medication that affects the neurotransmitters, even SAM-e, without monitoring by a doctor. It takes at least two weeks for MAO inhibitors to clear your body after you stop swallowing them, so you must continue to be careful during that period. Similarly, anyone who routinely takes illicit substances like heroin or cocaine should avoid SAM-e, since those drugs also affect the brain.

Finally, although no one has published any instance of bad reactions, women who are pregnant or nursing should avoid SAM-e, as they should any prescription drug or supplement, without the approval of their physician.

FOUR SUCCESS STORIES

Rasheeda has struggled with severe depression off and on for over thirty years, ever since she was a teenager. A mother of two teenage girls, she works intermittently as a legal secretary. During her good periods, which generally last for from two to five years, she is an active member of her local PTA and sings at her church. But during her dark moods, which can go on for up to twelve months, she withdraws from all activities. Rasheeda knows that her children are ultrasensitive to her moods, and she has sought treatment on numerous occasions. But prescription meds made her life excruciating. She hated the drowsiness, the headaches, and the insomnia. "Even when I am suicidal I will not ever take a drug," she insists.

One day she started feeling that old black cloud begin to hover over her again. After surfing the Internet, she came across references to SAM-e. What sold her was not only the lack of side effects but its quick action. "I was amazed when I noticed a difference in about five days," she reports. She did start becoming a little manic, she said, so she adjusted the dosage down to 800 mg (four pills) a day. Within a few weeks she stopped taking the supplement, and remained on an even keel. A few months later she called on SAM-e again to short-circuit her depression. "I am certain it works for me," she says.

.   .   .

Charlie, a self-employed auto mechanic, has always been the kind of guy who sees the glass as half empty. His somewhat cranky personality never prevented him from succeeding professionally, nor did it stop him from having a satisfying family life—until, that is, he fell into a deep funk that seemed to come out of nowhere. With an unhappy wife and a business that was sliding, Charlie sought help. He tried St. John's wort, but it didn't work. A psychiatrist prescribed the antidepressant Wellbutrin (bupropion), which makes some people agitated, and the antianxiety drug BuSpar (buspirone), which can be addictive over the long term—a common combination. "The combination worked well, and I used them for several months," Charlie recalls. There was just one problem: "I noticed impaired memory, which got worse," he says. His psychiatrist told him that Wellbutrin could have that effect, and suggested he replace the drug with SAM-e. Charlie was really surprised. "This psychiatrist is definitely not a proponent of alternative medicine."

Over the space of two weeks Charlie gradually cut the Wellbutrin down to nothing while starting on SAM-e, moving up to five pills (1,000 mg) a day. He also stopped taking BuSpar. It turned out that SAM-e alone provided the benefits of the two drugs—and without side effects or the risk of addiction. Charlie continued on SAM-e for an additional three months, then stopped. Although his memory never came back to what it was before, he is basically his normal, somewhat curmudgeonly self. He keeps some SAM-e in the medicine chest in case the depression ever returns.

.   .   .

For Rose, the truly despairing days were far back in her past—high school, a bad first marriage right after college, the anxiety of trying to figure out a career for herself. By age thirty, in her second marriage, she was subject to periods of malaise rather than the deep depression of her earlier years. Her life now revolved around her two children, a one-year-old and a two-and-a-half-year-old. Rose had really enjoyed her first daughter, but the second proved to be almost too much. The only time she had alone was late at night, when she read instead of getting much-needed sleep. To take care of the girls, Rose had cut short her graduate studies, and she worried that she would not catch up once her children were in school.

By each afternoon she was ready to climb into bed—but she couldn't because one child was always awake. Frazzled, testy, and exhausted most of the time, she just didn't know how to cope.

Then, at the suggestion of a friend, she tried SAM-e. Her situation didn't change much, but her mood did. "SAM-e is like caffeine without the jitters. I've become much more energetic and clear-headed. And I don't fade around three or four in the afternoon like I used to," reports Rose, who is now taking two pills (400 mg total) a day. Operating in a higher gear, Rose has found the energy to take one class, which makes her feel as if she is still operating in an adult world. She is happy that she is preparing for the future when her kids will be more self-sufficient.

For seven years Anna took Prozac to overcome the depression that had hampered her since she was an adolescent. And for seven years the sometime actress felt fine. But then the beneficial effects of the Prozac wore off, an uncommon though hardly unheard of occurrence. No juggling with the Prozac dosage by her doctor could stave off the depression, so he switched her to an older tricyclic drug, which she took for over a year. "I hated it. I felt cranky and sick all the time, and still was fairly depressed," she recalls.

Then she read a *Newsweek* article about SAM-e and decided, as she puts it, to "take the plunge." Under her doctor's supervision, she gradually cut down on the prescription antidepressant and added SAM-e, in increments of 200 mg each week. After three weeks she was off the prescription meds and was only taking 600 mg of SAM-e a day. "I haven't felt this good in years! And all those awful side effects are gone!" exclaims the forty-two-year-old.

HOW TO USE SAM-e

Although SAM-e is not a miracle cure—nothing is—it can be enormously helpful for people crippled by depression. The adequate dosage is a matter of controversy, however. In most studies on depression, SAM-e was given at the rate of 1,600 mg, or eight 200mg pills, a day. With pills costing somewhere around one dollar each, this calls for a substantial outlay of cash. Manufacturers generally recommend a much smaller dose, of two 200mg pills a day—still a lot of money but tolerable for many people. Within the alternative medicine field, some practitioners have questioned the manufacturer's recommendations, charging that they have cynically understated the correct dosage to avoid frightening away customers.

Whether the manufacturers are cynical or not, several practicing psychiatrists have found that the two-pill, 400mg daily dose works well for a fair number of people, especially those with mild to moderate depression. These doctors include Dr. Opler; Dr. Hyla Cass, a southern California psychiatrist and author of *St. John's Wort: Nature's Blues Buster* (Avery, 1998), and Dr. Richard Brown, a Columbia University psychiatry professor who is coauthor of the first big book on SAM-e, *Stop Depression Now* (Putnam, 1999). If the 400mg dose doesn't cause significant improvement in your mood after ten to fourteen days, the recommendation is to move up to 800 mg a day (four pills) for another ten to fourteen days. If you still don't see improvement, it's time to consult a medical professional, who may try another drug or a combination of drugs.

Since SAM-e depends on the presence of certain B vitamins to work, make sure that every morning you also take a B complex pill with the approximate recommended daily allowances for each micronutrient.

If you are already taking an antidepressant and want to switch to SAM-e (with your doctor's consent), make sure you withdraw from the prescription drug gradually. SSRIs, in particular, can produce unpleasant flu-like symptoms such as achiness, fatigue, nasal congestion, and headaches if they are abruptly terminated.

PIGGYBACKING ON OTHER ANTIDEPRESSANTS

In Italy, SAM-e is often used to lift people's moods quickly while they are waiting for other drugs like Elavil or Prozac to kick in.[4] In the United States some psychiatrists combine

SAM-e with different drugs to lower the dose, and hence the side effects that come with conventional antidepressants. Because these drugs require prescriptions, you could not make these combinations on your own. Nor would you want to, since expert advice is needed to ensure the safety and efficacy of the mix.

If you want to try a SAM-e combo, where would you turn for help? Unfortunately, it is hard to know which doctors are well versed in the natural supplement, although a surprising number of conventionally trained psychiatrists are amenable to using it. Your odds of finding a sympathetic doctor are improved if you look for one associated with the American Holistic Medical Association (access its Web site, www. holisticmedicine.org, or search in a local directory of alternative medicine practitioners).

On your own, you can combine St. John's wort, which can be mildly sedating, with SAM-e, which is mildly energizing. Dr. Cass provides a regimen: "Start with 900 mg a day of St. John's wort in divided doses of 300 mg three times a day or 450 mg twice a day. If this is not working after a few weeks, increase St. John's wort to 1200 mg a day. Then add SAM-e, 200 mg a day for a week, increasing after a week to 400 mg (200 mg twice a day). This safe combination can work well synergistically. Just watch out for any untoward symptoms— agitation, insomnia, headache—that might indicate excessive serotonin. Lower the dosage if these occur."

PEER SUPPORT

To find out how ordinary users determine dosage, log on to a discussion group aimed at people who take SAM-e for depression—www.delphi.com/samesupport/messages. You'll also find useful information on combining SAM-e with other anti-depressants, dealing with side effects, and getting the best price. Members of this group seem to really relish helping out people new to SAM-e.

Chapter 6

THE SECOND ACT:
LIFE AFTER DEPRESSION

If you are depressed, taking SAM-e can give you back a feeling of control. Odds are your mood will improve significantly and your energy level will rise. Does this mean that your life will then be perfect? Hardly. Although the best-selling book *Listening to Prozac,* by psychiatrist Peter D. Kramer (Penguin, 1997), gives a rapturous account of life changes possible with that drug, the truth is that antidepressants, including SAM-e, are often only the beginning of a healing process. What they do is get you out from under the dark cloud that is sapping all your energy or motivation so you can make positive changes or just go forth into the world and get on with your life. Whereas depression puts people into a downward spiral, getting out of depression can jump-start an upward spiral.

The shift is not necessarily automatic. John McManamy, who writes an informative weekly Internet column on depression (www.suite101/welcome.cfm/depression), eloquently cautions against assuming that a pill can solve all your problems.

McManamy wrote that people should "bear in mind how complex and subtle and downright mischievous depression actually is. Even if there is a magic bullet and even if that magic bullet is SAM-e, all your problems will hardly crumple overnight in the face of a pill-induced methylation onslaught. SAM-e is not retroactive. It will not replace your bad memories with good ones, nor will it take over the heavy lifting in changing sad thoughts to happy ones. But it may get you back on your feet again. It may, like more traditional antidepressants, bring you back from the living dead, and that certainly is a start."

Sometimes professionals can help you build on the strides you have made by taking SAM-e.

PROFESSIONAL SUPPORT

The two most common psychological treatment approaches used for people who experience depression are cognitive therapy and interpersonal therapy. Both usually last for a fairly short time, generally ten to twenty weeks, and focus on what is happening in your life right now, as opposed to your past. These therapists, unlike the relatively silent psychoanalysts of the past, are directive; they give feedback to their patients rather than waiting for the patients to come up with insights on their own.

If people have told you that your negative outlook gets in your way, you might benefit from cognitive therapy. This therapy, which was developed by psychiatrist Aaron Beck of the University of Pennsylvania, attempts to change how you interpret events—from a negative to a more positive slant. The idea is that always expecting the worst, taking everything personally, and assuming that people have the basest of motivations is distorted thinking. When the distortions are pointed out, the patient, in theory anyway, will view the world in a more positive, less depressed manner.

Say, for instance, that you don't get a job you applied for, a circumstance that would normally lead you to remind yourself of all your past failures and make you fall into a deep funk. A cognitive therapist might make you see that your past is filled with successes and that this missed shot is really an aberration. He or she may also help you realize that you are really better suited for other jobs and that you are now free to seek them. By itself, cognitive therapy, which has been well studied, is best for milder cases of depression. It is frequently used in conjunction with antidepressants, and the combination may be more effective in treating depression than either pills or therapy alone.

Interpersonal therapy, which was developed by the late Harvard psychiatrist Gerald Klerman and Columbia University psychologist Myrna Weissman, has been less well studied, but it also is effective at relieving mild depression and is often used in conjunction with antidepressants. Its goal is to help people establish and maintain better relationships with others. Since social isolation seems to bring on recurrences of depression, this kind of therapy can be a good investment in the future.

Some psychiatrists (M.D.'s with medical training) perform short-term therapy, but the practitioner is more often a psychologist (with a Ph.D. or the less academically oriented Psy.D.), a social worker (with an M.S.W., usually from a two-year master's program), a psychiatric nurse (an R.N., who may have advanced training beyond college), or some other type of counselor. With the advent of managed care, many people find that their choice of therapist is limited to whoever is on their insurance plan's list. Many of these therapists are quite competent, but others are just starting out and have less experience. Go for an experienced practitioner if you have a choice; as in any other profession, veterans are usually much more skilled than novices.

You will probably not know from someone's credentials how good a match you will make. So interview some possibilities, if possible, until you feel comfortable. Comfort level is very important. Research says that the effectiveness of therapy has less to do with a practitioner's dogma than with the bond that develops between patient and therapist. If you feel that a therapist is caring and on your side, you will reap much more benefit from your visits.

There are also many ways to improve your life without professional help.

STAVING OFF STRESS

Chronic stress, of course, can make you miserable and torpedo your health. A two-pronged strategy can keep it within manageable limits. One tack is to reduce the stressors. A second tack is to increase your ability to handle the stress that's left.

Much stress these days comes from the unmanageable schedule—too much to do in too little time. The problem is especially acute for working mothers, who often enter a second shift, having to cook for their families and deal with their children's demands, when they come home from work. A well-designed study by psychologist Dr. Reed Larson of the University of Illinois found that the two busiest times of the week for working mothers in this country are from 5:00 to 7:00 P.M. on weekdays and all day on Saturdays, when they cram in all the errands they couldn't get to while at work.[1]

You don't have to be a working mom to be overbooked. In

the last ten years, we Americans have added 185 hours a year to our jobs. At 1,966 hours a year of work we have passed the supposedly workaholic Japanese to become the hardest-working employees in the world. And we don't get much of a break: Americans have fewer vacation days than people in any European country. Suburban people lose additional time—three or more hours a day—due to extraordinarily long commutes, often through irritatingly slow traffic. And many parents devote their spare time to driving their children from one activity to another.

One way to get some more free time and to stop feeling as if you're living in a pressure cooker, is to drop some tasks. Make a list of all the non-work-related activities you do each week, and see which ones provide the least satisfaction. If, for instance, you do not enjoy cleaning your house, you could pay someone else to do it, negotiate with your husband and children to pitch in, or lower your expectations. You may also be able to streamline your job by delegating some of your tasks to subordinates or by exchanging job responsibilities with a co-worker.

There are several ways to increase your ability to handle unavoidable stress. One is to practice a relaxation technique such as meditation or deep breathing for at least ten to fifteen minutes each day. Research has shown that the consistent use of a relaxation technique—they're all equally effective; just do the one that feels natural—help buffer people from stress. In fact, a group of studies by psychologist Dr. William Morgan of the University of Wisconsin suggests that taking *any* break from daily responsibilities—meditating or relaxing in an easy chair or planting seeds—can significantly lower stress.[2] For an encyclopedic listing of stress-reduction techniques, see *Stress Management: A Comprehensive Guide to Wellness,* by Edward A. Charlesworth and Ronald G. Nathan (Ballantine, 1985), or consult the immensely popular *Instant Calm,* by Australian businessman-turned-guru Paul Wilson (Penguin, 1995).

It is equally important to get enough sleep. When you are low on slumber, you are more affected by the annoying events of your life—just think of how cranky little kids are when they are sleepy. The National Sleep Foundation estimates that the average American suffers a shortfall in sleep of one hour each work night. While you can bounce back from one night of inadequate rest, to consistently shortchange yourself means that you are always operating at a sub-par level. Don't try to gain extra time by cutting out sleep; you are less efficient when you're tired and you're also more prone to anxiety and depression, say sleep researchers.

Another way to protect yourself from stress is to build in at least one pleasurable activity a day. A recent study by Dr. Jackie Gollan, a psychologist at Brown University Medical School, found that relapses into depression were much less common in patients who did things they enjoyed.[3] For life to be satisfying, you need reasons to look forward to getting out of bed in the morning. That may seem obvious, but many people focus on what they must do rather than what they would like to do.

EXERCISE: ANOTHER ANTIDEPRESSION STRATEGY

A large body of research says that consistent exercise can relieve, and probably help prevent, moderate and mild depression.[4] Heart-thumping aerobic exercise (such as fast walking, running, or swimming) and non-aerobic exercise (such as weight lifting) can improve your mood. When you are feeling down, just one ten-minute brisk walk (fast enough so you're breathing hard) will lower stress and help energize you, though longer sessions of twenty to thirty minutes are even better.

Many people believe that exercise produces a natural high in the form of endorphins, but research has not borne out this theory. Instead, various forms of exercise seem to remove stress chemicals like cortisol from the bloodstream. Done regularly— almost every day for twenty to thirty minutes a shot—exercise seems to help buffer the effects of stress. It also makes it easier to fall asleep and improves the quality of your slumber.

Of course, when you are depressed and low on energy, about the last thing you want to do is work out. So how do you motivate yourself to move? One method is to remind yourself of how good you're going to feel afterward, and then simply use willpower to get started. Another is to exercise in a social environment you find appealing. You may not feel like working up a sweat, but you'll go outside because you enjoy chatting with your walking partner. Or you can listen to something pleasant—like music you love—while you do something not so entertaining, like pedaling a stationary bike.

WILL YOU MISS THE DEPRESSION?

It happens. People who have been depressed most of their lives may find that they are uncomfortable with their unfamiliar, sunnier selves. Somewhat like people who have just been released after a long prison term, some formerly depressed people feel as if they have landed in a new country where, quite to their surprise, all the rules are different. Disoriented by the changes, they may go through a period of intense distress that may end quickly—or take years to subside. Newly recovered folks may feel dissatisfied with situations they put up with for years. They may want to make up for time lost to depression, or perhaps they'll find themselves in jobs that are beneath their talents. Relationships can become strained because the equilibrium comes apart when one partner changes.

How common is this "uplift anxiety," as the *New York Times* has called it?[5] "It's not a rare occurrence," one Harvard psychiatrist told the *Times,* "and it's not a very frequent occurrence. I think it's something in between."

Change is often unsettling. Most people feel liberated when their depression lifts after taking SAM-e or another drug. But it is also normal to have difficulty adjusting to a new mental state. Just remember: antidepressants are the beginning, not the end, of the repair process.

HOW LONG SHOULD YOU STAY ON SAM-e?

This is a tricky question to answer because everyone is different. You may recall from Chapter 3 that those who suffer from depression tend to be biochemically different from other people and so are susceptible to recurring episodes. To avoid relapse, it is generally recommended that a person with major depression continue antidepressant treatment for nine to twelve months, says Dr. Bruce Kagan. Patients who have had three or more episodes of severe depression should continue treatment indefinitely; otherwise they risk sinking into their dark moods again. And Dr. Kagan says that "People with chronic depres-

THE SECOND ACT: LIFE AFTER DEPRESSION

sion or dysthymia are likely to require chronic treatment." In other words, if your bleak moods have been relentless for years, you may need to stay on SAM-e for quite some time.

After a patient goes off an antidepressant, Dr. Lewis Opler reviews with him or her the warning signs that signal the beginning of a depressive episode. "For some patients," he says, "low energy preceded depression; for others, free-floating anxiety; for others, not enjoying things as much." These tip-offs are an indication that you should begin to take SAM-e again.

Whether you use SAM-e indefinitely or call upon it when you are especially in need, you can rest assured that it has an impeccable safety record. Even better: SAM-e is actually good for you. One of the best reasons to take the nutraceutical is that it helps not just depression but a number of other ailments as well, as you will learn in the succeeding chapters.

Chapter 7

THE ACHING JOINTS OF OSTEOARTHRITIS

Osteoarthritis seems almost as inevitable as death and taxes. The older you get, the more likely you are to experience it. By age seventy, almost all Americans show the wear and tear on their joints that can lead to the pain and stiffness of this most common form of arthritis. For unknown reasons, women are about twice as likely as men to experience symptoms of the disease. All told, 21 million Americans, about half of them under age sixty-five, suffer from clinical, or symptomatic, osteo-arthritis. And as baby boomers continue to cross the half-century mark, these numbers will keep on growing.

Many lucky people have no symptoms whatsoever of joint damage (doctors believe that these asymptomatic people do not require treatment), but millions of others with osteoarthritic joints are hobbled by stiffness and pain. On bad days, walking to the store, cooking dinner, and even opening the mail may be beyond them. Even on good days, relentless pain may wear them down. Depression is very common among arthritis sufferers.

Conventional medicine has not come close to finding a cure for osteoarthritis, nor has it done a good job of alleviating its symptoms. It is thus not surprising that an enormous number of osteoarthritis sufferers—84 percent in one sample of patients of rheumatologists—turn to alternative medicine, such as SAM-e, for relief.[1]

ANATOMY OF A JOINT

Arthritis literally means an inflammation of the joints—from the Greek "arth" (joint) and "itis" (inflammation). To comprehend the illness, you need to understand the structure of your joints.

Bones hold you up, but joints allow you to move. Situated where two bones meet, joints make it possible for you to bend, swivel, and rotate your body. Some joints are very simple, like the hinges in your fingers, while others are biomechanical marvels like the ball-and-socket apparatus of your hips. Without functioning joints, you would not be able to walk, hold a fork, or pick up a baby. But joints are potentially vulnerable to damage by impact or friction.

Each joint is protected and enclosed by a joint capsule. This tough shell, made of protein fibers called collagen, is attached to bones on either side and helps stabilize the joint. Lining the joint capsule is a thin wall called the synovial membrane. It secretes synovial fluid, which lubricates the joint—rather like oil in a car engine—and fills up the small space around and between the bones. To further protect against friction, the end of each bone is covered by stiff, shock-absorbing cartilage. Much of the research on osteoarthritis focuses on this articular (which means "joint") cartilage. Studies on cadaver hands have found that the high water content of cartilage is what allows it to cushion mechanical stress. Under ordinary conditions, articular cartilage repairs itself through secretions from specialized cells named chondrocytes. Cartilage contains no blood vessels, so it is nourished by the synovial fluid.

Just outside the joint are muscles, ligaments (connective tissue that binds bone to bone), and tendons (connective tissue that links bone to muscle). They keep the joint aligned, provide further support, and help bones move properly. The health of the joints depends largely on the strength of this support system.

For most of our lives, our joints function according to plan. As we grow older, however, there is more chance that something will go wrong.

THE BIG SNAFU

Osteoarthritis is sometimes known as the wear-and-tear arthritis. In a joint afflicted by this disorder, the cartilage and other tissues break down, presumably because of year-after-year damage that becomes unfixable, generally starting around age forty-five. In the early stages, the two smooth cartilage surfaces on the ends of the bones become pitted and softer as they make contact with each other. At first, the cartilage is able to replace most of the missing cells. But the repairs become overwhelming, and eventually large sections of cartilage may be worn away completely. With the cushioning reduced, you may experience pain and reduced mobility when you try to move the joint.

As the osteoarthritis progresses, your bones change shape. The bone ends thicken and form spurs along the sides where ligaments and the joint capsule are connected to the bone. These spurs, or osteophytes, form lumps that are especially noticable in the fingers of people with arthritis. Ligaments can thicken, too. Cartilage becomes softer and softer; its water content increases. Small pieces of loose bone or cartilage, called joint mice, may float in the joint space, irritating the lining or synovial membrane and contributing to the pain that comes with movement.

In severe osteoarthritis, there is almost no articular cartilage left. Bone ends rub against each other in the joint, causing pain and making movement next to impossible. People who reach this stage, especially when the damage is in their hips, can often be helped only by joint-replacement surgery.

There is a big discrepancy between the physical signs of osteoarthritis and the actual experience of symptoms. Only about one-quarter of people whose X-rays show sign of joint damage feel pain and endure stiffness. Mild cases of osteo-arthritis may cause no pain, and many people, especially those whose arthritis is limited to their hands, never develop an advanced case of the disorder. The disease is not likely to go away, however, and is generally progressive. A few people experience deterioration quickly, but it is more common for additional damage to slowly develop each year.

The joints most often affected by this condition are those in the hips, knees, hands, and feet. Osteoarthritis is also common in parts of the spine, especially the lower back and the neck. Disks between the vertebrae are made of cartilage, and they start to wear out, just like the cartilage in other joints, narrow-ing the spaces between the vertebrae. You lose height when this happens to several disks. If the bone spurs caused by osteo-arthritis impinge on nerves in the spine, the condition can be extremely painful.

Some joints are fairly immune to osteoarthritis. The ankles, wrists, and elbows rarely show evidence of osteoarthritis, unless they have been subject to injury or extreme stress.

WHAT'S GOING WRONG?

For many years there was little research interest in osteoarthritis. It was just considered an inevitable part of aging—unfortunate but unfixable. In the last decade or so, however, a flurry of scientific activity has yielded new preventive measures, new treatments, and new insights. "We are at the cusp of discovery and improvement," said Dr. David T. Felson, of Boston University School of Medicine's Multipurpose Arthritis and Musculoskeletal Diseases Center, at a scientific conference on osteoarthritis sponsored by the National Institute of Arthritis and Musculoskeletal and Skin Diseases in the summer of 1999.[2]

The big question is a seemingly simple one: what causes osteoarthritis? Surprisingly, no one really knows.

A propensity for the illness does appear to be inherited. Studies comparing fraternal and identical twins estimate that 39 to 54 percent of the variability in osteoarthritis is due to genetics. But there doesn't seem to be an arthritis gene per se; rather, a number of genes are probably involved. People, for instance, may be born with misaligned joints (rates of osteoarthritis are high in those with abnormally developed hips) or with defective cartilage.

Stress on the joints seems to take a big toll, too. One study has found that workers whose job entails prolonged or repeated knee bending—squatting, kneeling, or climbing many flights of stairs—are significantly more likely than other employees to develop arthritis in the knees.[3] Similarly, research has shown that physical laborers tend to develop this disease in the dominant (usually right) hand. Among athletes, the joint most affected is often the one most used—feet and ankles in ballet dancers, shoulders and elbows in baseball pitchers, and knees in football players. People who have injured joints by, say, spraining an ankle, are also prone to develop osteoarthritis in that spot. And obese people are much more likely than others to become arthritic in the knees and, to a lesser extent, the hips, probably because of the excess burden on their joints.

Stress and misalignments are just part of the story. Clearly, some malfunction or, more likely, set of malfunctions, causes the deterioration of the articular cartilage. One theory focuses on enzymes released by the cartilage cells and the synovial membrane. When these are in the right balance, they break down and renew cartilage at the appropriate rate. But if they go out of balance—for unknown reasons—they destroy this network faster than it is regenerated. Researchers are also looking at changes in the bone beneath the cartilage during osteoarthritis. It is, writes the British researcher Paul Dieppe, "quite clear that osteoarthritis is a disorder of the whole synovial joint organ, not just the cartilage. Indeed, the articular cartilage may be the innocent bystander of a disease process that is centered more in bone than in cartilage—a large body of evidence on the importance of bone turnover in progressive osteoarthritis is accumulating."[4]

CAN YOU PREVENT OSTEOARTHRITIS?

Many of the risks for osteoarthritis are unchangeable. If you are alive and you anticipate growing older, you stand a good chance of developing clinical osteoarthritis—OA that you can notice. Your risk increases enormously as you get grayer. At age forty-four, only 2 percent of Americans experience some symptoms. For those between forty-five and sixty-four, the figure rises to 30 percent. By retirement age—sixty-five and over—the figure jumps to around 65 percent.

Sex is also a contributor. Women, overall, constitute 74 percent of people affected by osteoarthritis. Up until the age of fifty, however, the number of women and men sufferers is almost equal, a fact that has led scientists to question whether the hormone estrogen, which is present in women until menopause, has a protective effect. And some epidemiological studies do suggest that using estrogen replacement therapy after menopause helps. Analysis of a subset of data from the large-scale Framingham Study, which is famous for providing information on cardiovascular disease, showed a 60 percent reduction in the incidence and progression of osteoarthritis in the knee among older white women who were using estrogen replacement therapy.[5] But previous use of such therapy offered no protection. So women who are trying to decide whether or not to take estrogen have another item to put in the "benefits" column.

Race and ethnicity are also associated with the odds of developing osteoarthritis and of becoming disabled by it. African-Americans are more likely than whites to develop the disorder, and both African-Americans and Hispanics report greater disability from the ailment.

These differences may stem in part from the somewhat greater prevalence of obesity among these two groups. Obesity—a modifiable risk—increases the chances of developing arthritis in the knees and, less so, the hips, especially in women. In 1999, Dr. Felson estimated that eliminating obesity in the United States would result in a 25 to 50 percent drop in osteoarthritis (OA) of the knees and a 25 percent reduction in OA of the hips. The problem with obesity seems to be not just extra weight but also excess fat tissue, which may produce hormones or growth factors that make cartilage and the underlying bone more susceptible to OA.

Chronic stress on the joints, as mentioned earlier, predisposes you to OA, but physical inactivity also carries big risks. Strong muscles help keep joints aligned and protect against undue stress. Researchers at Indiana University School of Medicine have found that weak quadriceps muscles, which are in the front of the thighs and help stabilize knees, are a precursor of knee OA in women.[6] Knee pain can be reduced by strengthening this muscle. Thus, to some extent, you can lower your risk of getting OA by keeping your weight in line and by doing moderate-impact exercise like jogging rather than sudden-impact exercise like soccer or football.

But if you are reading this chapter, you probably already suspect you have OA. How do you know for certain? Since there are no blood tests for the disorder, a diagnosis is generally made on the basis of your symptoms—and by ruling out the similar-seeming rheumatoid arthritis.

ARE YOU SURE IT'S OA?

There are over one hundred forms of arthritis, but the vast majority of sufferers have either osteoarthritis or rheumatoid arthritis, the second most common type. Although the two kinds can cause similar symptoms of pain and stiffness, it is important to get a medical diagnosis. Osteoarthritis and rheumatoid arthritis (RA) respond to different kinds of medication. (SAM-e, for instance, is appropriate only for OA.) There is a big advantage to getting rheumatoid arthritis treated right away: current thinking is that aggressive treatment in the early stages will significantly slow down the progression of the disease.

Rheumatoid arthritis, which afflicts about 2.1 million adult Americans, is an autoimmune disease in which your body's immune system goes haywire. White blood cells, instead of attacking intruders such as bacteria, strike the synovial membrane that lines your joints. Inflamed and thickened, the membrane produces excess fluid, causing the joint to become swollen, warm, tender, and painful to move. As the disease progresses, chemicals released from the blood cells and the synovial membrane consume cartilage, bone, tendon, and ligament tissues around the joint. Eventually the joint becomes misshapen and may cease to function. Over the long run, painful and debilitating flare-ups are likely to alternate with periods of remission in which sufferers feel relatively comfortable.

Rheumatoid arthritis, which generally strikes people between the ages of twenty-five and fifty, is considered a more serious illness than osteoarthritis, which usually doesn't affect people until age forty or older and in which the discomfort is limited to specific joint areas. Rheumatoid arthritis is more of a whole-body disease that can cause people to feel sick all over, to be exhausted, and to have a fever, lose weight, and generally feel achy. Unlike OA, which tends to develop gradually over the years, RA can start quite quickly, within a matter of weeks or months. The joints of an RA patient become red, warm, and, in advanced cases, very misshapen. In addition, RA tends to affect joints on both sides of the body—both hands, for example—while OA normally begins with isolated joints or joints only on one side of the body.

It is believed that most of the damage occurs within the first two years of the onset of rheumatoid arthritis, making early diagnosis and treatment imperative. If you suspect rheumatoid arthritis, run, don't walk, to a physician. In addition to examining your joints (the damage from RA looks different from that of OA), the doctor will likely perform two tests: erythrocyte sedimentation rate (known as sed rate), which indicates some kind of inflammation in the body, and a test for an antibody called rheumatoid factor, which is present in four out of five RA sufferers. Results of both tests are usually negative for someone with osteoarthritis, leading the way for the right kind of treatment.

CONVENTIONAL MEDICATIONS FOR OSTEOARTHRITIS: LOTS OF PROBLEMS

Relieving discomfort is a major objective of medications, since research shows that most of the disability from osteoarthritis is due to the pain of moving joints rather than their mechanical malfunctioning. Aspirin, which has been on the U.S. market since 1899, is the first drug that many people take for OA. It is part of a larger group of medications called nonsteroidal anti-inflammatory drugs, or NSAIDs (pronounced EN-sedz), of which Advil (ibuprofen) is one of the best known. These drugs, especially in their stronger prescription versions, reduce both pain and swelling. They do so largely by interfering with the synthesis of internal chemicals called prostaglandins.

Wholesale stifling of prostaglandins is a double-edged sword, however, because these hormone-like substances come in two forms: one that produces inflammation and a second that allows for the making of the mucus that lines the stomach and intestinal tract. This lining protects the digestive tract from the effects of stomach acid and other harsh chemicals. When prostaglandins of both types are inhibited, inflammation in the body is reduced but the digestive tract is subject to the corrosive effects of our own digestive juices.

Aspirin, which harms the stomach lining directly as well as indirectly through the suppression of prostaglandins, has the most damaging effect on the digestive tract. Heavy users of this nonprescription drug face a serious risk of developing ulcers, or holes in the stomach lining, which can cause dangerous bleeding. Risks are lower for other NSAIDs. Yet about one-fifth of long-term users of all these drugs experience an ulcer. Each year complications from NSAIDs treatment result in an estimated 41,000 hospital admissions and 3,300 deaths. Chronic use also increases your chances of developing kidney and liver disease. Worst of all, some kinds of NSAIDs appear to make cartilage deteriorate—not exactly what you're looking for in an arthritis treatment.[7]

Introduced in 1998, the newest variation on the NSAIDs theme, Celebrex (celecoxib) significantly reduces the risk of gastrointestinal problems. Celebrex and its near cousin Vioxx (rofecoxib), introduced in mid-1999, inhibit only the prostaglandin pathway dealing with inflammation, which means that the prostaglandins that protect the digestive tract can continue to do their job. The runaway success of Celebrex—over 12 million prescriptions were written in its first year, exceeding the spectacular debut of the anti-impotence drug Viagra (sildenafil citrate)—attests to the high demand for an arthritis medication without serious side effects.

Yet these so-called Cox-2 inhibitors work no better than other NSAIDs in reducing pain and inflammation, and studies have suggested that their high cost (around $2.50 a day) may not be justified for people at low risk for gastrointestinal complications. You are at high risk if you have already experienced heartburn, stomach pain, nausea, or vomiting with NSAIDs or if you have had an ulcer. For a nifty on-line risk assessment, call up www.seniors.org/score, written by Dr. Gurkirpal Singh, an immunologist and rheumatologist with Stanford University Medical Center.

The American College of Rheumatology believes that Americans with osteoarthritis should avoid gastrointestinal risks by using acetaminophen, best known as the brand Tylenol. Acetaminophen reduces pain by a different pathway than the NSAIDs and does not affect the prostaglandins—meaning that it does not harm your stomach but also does not relieve inflammation. Since inflammation is not as big a problem for OA sufferers as it is for RA patients, the pain relief from acetaminophen may well be sufficient. This over-the-counter drug comes with its own risks, however. In long-term users it may cause kidney and liver problems. People who have more than three alcoholic drinks a day are at especial risk for liver damage.

Medications known as cortisteroids are used for short-term pain relief in osteoarthritis. These are synthetic versions of an anti-inflammatory chemical that occurs naturally in the body. Oral cortisteroids, which are routinely taken by some people with asthma, have many serious side effects, like weight gain, easy bruising, bone-thinning (osteoporosis), and high blood pressure, to name only a few. While oral cortisteroids are sometimes necessary for people with rheumatoid arthritis, they are uncalled for with OA sufferers. But doctors may occasionally stop joint pain with injections of cortisteroids, which have much less potential for producing side effects. The relief is effective, but generally lasts for only a few months and is not suitable for hip joints, where the appropriate injection site is hard to locate. Because it is possible, though unlikely, that the injection will cause an infection within the joint, physicians limit them to only a few times a year.

If you're thinking that there must be a better way, you're right. A safer alternative does exist: SAM-e, as we shall see in the next chapter, not only reduces the pain of osteoarthritis effectively and safely but—unlike conventional medications—may also help improve to repair joint damage.

Chapter 8

NATURAL BORN PAINKILLER: SAM-e FOR ARTHRITIS RELIEF

As a teenager, Suzanne was told to expect trouble sooner or later after she had surgery fusing together two of the vertebrae in her lower back. She didn't anticipate, however, that crippling pain in her legs would suddenly strike eighteen years later. The pain probably came from arthritic vertebrae pressing on the sciatic nerve that runs from the base of the spine to the feet. Suzanne also experienced soreness in several other joints, including the hips and the knees. For ten months Suzanne, a thirty-five-year-old mother of three, was in agony. "The doctor was giving me up to 60 mg of morphine a day, and I was still in pain, not to mention losing all motivation in life from being drugged," she recalls.

Then a friend suggested that she try SAM-e. "I was reducing the amount of pain meds within a week, before I had finished my first box of twenty tablets. I take 400 mg a day, mostly in the morning," Suzanne says. She no longer needs morphine, and is back to being active in the PTA and other community affairs. "SAM-e changed my life when I was about to give up on the pain war," asserts Suzanne.

SAM-e'S BENEFITS: REDUCED PAIN AND STIFFNESS

The discovery of SAM-e as an arthritis treatment is one of those eureka experiences that make science so dramatic. In the late 1970s, an Italian researcher was doing clinical trials to test the efficacy of SAM-e as an antidepressant, which was then available only in an injectable form. Some of the patients reported a totally unexpected side effect—they got relief from the pain of osteoarthritis. And so another group of Italian researchers set out to see how well SAM-e worked as an alternative to the nonsteroidal anti-inflammatory drug ketoprofen (now sold over the counter in the United States as Orudis KT). SAM-e seemed promising because it was already known not to interfere with the protective mucous lining of the gastrointestinal tract; unlike NSAIDs such as ketoprofen and aspirin, it does not damage the stomach and cause ulcers. And researchers had already shown in animals that SAM-e has anti-inflammatory and analgesic (pain-relieving) properties. The analgesic effects of SAM-e apparently do not involve the prostaglandins pathway that makes NSAIDs effective but also cause their gastrointestinal side effects.

This early research found SAM-e as effective as ketoprofen. The findings held up in later research, most done after scientists had learned to put SAM-e into a stable pill form. SAM-e consistently performed better than placebos and as well as various NSAIDs—but without the side effects. In one study of 734 patients with osteoarthritis of the hip, knee, spine, and hand, a 1,200mg oral dose of SAM-e for twenty-eight days reduced symptoms as effectively as did a 750mg dose of naproxen (Aleve), but both patients and their doctors reported that SAM-e was easier to tolerate and produced fewer side effects.[1]

The largest study published in English, with more than 20,000 subjects, found a "very good" or "good" outcome in over 70 percent of patients who took SAM-e for symptoms of osteoarthritis.[2] It should be mentioned, however, that this was an open study, meaning that it involved no control group. Nonetheless, the evidence of favor of SAM-e's pain-relieving benefits is strong, and in 1999 the conservative Arthritis Foundation issued a favorable position statement: "Arthritis Foundation medical experts feel that there is sufficient information to support the claim that SAM-e provides pain relief."[3]

More controversial is the assertion that SAM-e can help heal damaged cartilage. Cartilage has three major components: collagen, a network of connective tissue; proteoglycan, huge molecules outside the collagen that attract and hold water; and chondrocytes, the manufacturing centers of the operation, which make, among other things, the two other components of cartilage. Chondrocytes are embedded in the cartilage network and cannot operate unless energy in the form of glucose reaches them. But when cartilage is impaired, glucose has trouble meeting up with the chondrocytes. Thus, in the downward spiral set off by osteoarthritis, the very cells that could replace damaged tissue are themselves malfunctioning.

A series of lab and animal studies suggest that SAM-e can stimulate the retention of protogylcans, increase chondrocytes, and generally reduce damage to cartilage.[4] Researchers believe that part of the pain-relieving effect of SAM-e comes from its ability to lessen the malfunctioning of osteoarthritic joints. In at least one study, patients continued to feel symptom relief well up to two and a half months after ending their SAM-e regimen—a finding which implies that the supplement causes structural improvement.[5] At the very least, it is clear that

SAM-e, unlike NSAIDs and cortisteroids, is chondroprotec-tive—that is, it does no damage to the chondrocytes and hence to the cartilage in joints. SAM-e has other advantages over NSAIDs. It does not harm the gastrointestinal tract and, as we shall see in Chapter 10, will not hurt and probably helps the liver, which is likely to be damaged in people who take NSAIDs and acetaminophen for many years. And SAM-e, regardless of its direct effect on cartilage, is well known to pro-vide anti-inflammatory and analgesic benefits.

GETTING THE MOST OUT OF SAM-e

Most research on SAM-e has used a daily regimen of 1,200 mg or higher. But with a much smaller dosage, a two-year German study achieved a marked decline in symptoms, including stiff-ness in the morning, limitation in movement, pain at rest, and pain in movement.[6] In this study, the patients received 600 mg of SAM-e (equal to three 200mg tablets) a day for two weeks, then 400 mg a day (two tablets) for the rest of the study period. And for many people, this 400mg dosing may well be adequate for achieving relief (this dosage may also relieve depression, as it did in the German study).

Take the case of Jim, a thirty-seven-year-old sales represen-tative for a large manufacturing firm and a former star school athlete, who has been intermittently crippled by joint pain and stiffness for the last decade and a half. He has almost elimi-nated his joint pain and stiffness with a dose of just 200 mg a day of SAM-e. Before taking SAM-e, he used a nonsteroidal anti-inflammatory drug called Indocin (indomethacin), which caused his stomach to bleed. SAM-e, with its promise of no side effects, held a great deal of appeal. "My shoulders hurt so bad that I couldn't throw a bone to my dog overhand—I had to do it underhand," says Jim. "But after taking SAM-e for seven months, I started playing tennis again. I used to hit a screamer of a serve, and I've almost got it back. I'm really grateful for the improvement because we just had a baby. I need to be active so I can keep up with the kid."

But don't expect arthritis aches to go away immediately, as a headache does when you swallow aspirin; it may be two weeks before you feel better. Just remember to take a vitamin B complex pill with about the minimum daily values each day.

And bear in mind that osteoarthritis is progressive and chronic. So far, there is no cure. You can reduce your pain and stiffness with SAM-e, avoid the side effects of NSAIDs, and possibly improve the health of your joints. But SAM-e is only one part of the solution. You need a three-pronged approach to prevent further damage. You need to exercise, maintain a reasonable weight, and get certain vitamins.

THE IMPORTANCE OF EXERCISE

Like bones and muscles, joints are in a constant state of renewal. Also like bones and muscles, your joints need stimulation. Pressure on them—the kind of recurring loading that happens when you walk or run—is useful because it helps them absorb nutrients from the synovial fluid that fills the empty spaces within the joint structure. Loading also sparks the synthesis of proteoglycans, a component of cartilage. In addition, movement helps keep the surrounding ligaments, tendons, and muscles strong. These are needed to support and stabilize your joints. If they become weak, your joints have to carry more than their fair share of the load, setting you up for further damage.

Unfortunately, when you feel achy and stiff, exercise is about the last thing on your mind. And for years, doctors used to recommend that osteoarthritis sufferers take it easy. They believed that working out would only increase wear and tear on the joints. But studies on animals have confirmed that immobilizing the joints actually makes arthritis worse. Fewer proteoglycans are produced, resulting in a higher water content in the cartilage that buffers the two bones that meet at the joint. This articular (joint) cartilage becomes softer, thinner, and pitted, continuing its downward spiral.

These days, doctors recommend exercise for people with osteoarthritis. A number of studies back them up. According to a 1999 review of several research efforts, exercise programs can reduce pain, lower disability, and generally make patients with osteoarthritis in the hips and knees feel better.[7] Why do they feel better? Because exercise relaxes muscles, ameliorates muscle spasms, and increases blood flow to joints.

Exercise, of course, comes in a variety pack. Aerobic exercise, the kind that gets your heart thumping fast, has been the best studied. Endurance activities like brisk walking, swimming, and cycling strengthen your heart and lungs and improve your stamina. Doing these activities consistently reduces your risks of heart attacks, high blood pressure, diabetes, colon cancer (and possibly breast cancer), depression, and anxiety. This kind of exercise also burns a lot of calories, useful for anyone who needs to lose weight.

Resistance training, which builds specific muscles through lifting weights or using targeted gym equipment, is especially good at improving muscle strength and reducing your chances of getting osteoporosis, a disease that's especially dangerous for people whose joints are already weakened by arthritis. Building up your quadriceps muscles, those on the front of your thighs, seems to be especially important in protecting your knees from further damage and for reducing pain. Strength-training workouts of all sorts also cut down on anxiety, and they probably increase your metabolic rate, too. The reasoning goes like this: Muscles are more metabolically active than fat stores. If you become more muscular you increase the number of calories your body burns each day (your basal metabolic rate) just sustaining your inner workings. Thus, if you build up your muscles, and don't change how much you eat, you can expect to lose a few pounds slowly over a year.

People with limited mobility caused by osteoarthritis can gain some of the benefits of resistance training by doing exercises while seated in their chairs. To find out more about these exercises and about special classes and videotapes for arthritis sufferers, contact your local Arthritis Foundation office (check your local phone book or call the national office at 404-872-7100 or 800-283-7800).

Which kind of exercise is best for someone with OA, aerobic or resistance? The answer: both are fine. A relatively large-scale study (almost 450 participants) of people with knee osteoarthritis age sixty and over found that the benefits were similar whether the subjects did an aerobic activity or a weight-training program.[8] You can do one kind or another—but ideally both—depending on your preference.

Exercise need not be intense. Moderate exercise, like walking or gardening, is adequate for improving your health and is easier for many people with OA to tolerate. And you don't need to do it in one shot. Research has shown that you can get as much benefit from taking three ten-minute walks a day as one thirty-minute walk. This is a realistic plan of action for times when you have flare-ups and need to rest after short periods of exertion. But if you plan on breaking up your exercise this way, it is very helpful to list all your activity in a log. Otherwise it is easy to lose count of how many times you're exercising each day. For advice on setting up your own program, consult the excellent book *Fit over Forty* (William Morrow, 1996), by Tufts University cardiologist James M. Rippe.

Stretching to maintain and increase your range of motion is also crucial to the health of your joints. People with osteoarthritis are often inflexible, especially in their lower halves. This inflexibility contributes to pain, difficulty moving, and an increased risk of falling. Stretching exercises take your joints to the edge of their comfortable limits, then go a little further, to increase mobility. By compressing your joints they also stimulate the repair and regrowth of the articular cartilage.

Swimming is a real bargain exercise. It provides all three types of exercise movements at once: you get an aerobic workout, you do resistance training by moving your body against water, and you stretch as you extend your arms and legs. Better yet, the water holds you up so that you don't feel the weight of your body on the joints. Some people with advanced osteoarthritis say they feel their best in the water. Water exercise classes, widely available at YMCAs and YWCAs, often in conjunction with the Arthritis Foundation, offer similar benefits for those who like the water but do not enjoy swimming. These classes, even when held in health clubs, tend not to attract a younger crowd and so are comfortable for people who remember when Eisenhower was in office.

Before you begin exercising, especially if you are a novice, it's useful to consult an expert who can tailor-make a routine around your specific needs. Physical therapists are specialists in the workings of the muscles and joints. After assessing your strengths and weaknesses, they will show you how to exercise optimally in two- to three-times-a-week sessions, generally of around forty-five minutes. The therapists may also employ devices and procedures like ice packs, heating pads, massage, ultrasound and TENS (transcutaneous electrical nerve stimulation, which produces a mild electrical current that shuts off muscle spasms) to reduce your pain and increase mobility. When a physician refers you to a physical therapist the cost is often reimbursed by insurance companies; they understand that OA patients who exercise will cost them less in the long run.

After physical therapy, and sometimes instead of it, patients may turn to certified exercise specialists—personal trainers with advanced training that equips them to handle chronic conditions like arthritis. Less hands-on than physical therapists— they are, for instance, unlikely to massage you—they are like personal coaches who set up and take you through an exercise routine. Often they are attached to hospitals or pain clinics, and some come right to your home. Look for someone who has been certified by a national training organization. The most stringent programs are offered by the American College of Sports Medicine in Indianapolis and the Cooper Institute for Aerobics Research in Dallas.

REDUCING YOUR LOAD: TIPS ON LOSING WEIGHT

Obesity is a well-known risk for osteoarthritis, especially in the knees but also in the hips and possibly in the hands. The danger is presumed to stem from the high stress on the joints. Internal chemicals stimulated by the presence of extra fat tissue may also cause havoc. But there's good news: if you are overweight, a fairly small weight loss—just 10 or so pounds—can significantly reduce your chances of developing OA, at least in the knees.[9] This amount of weight loss also dramatically improves your health by also lowering your chances of developing heart disease and diabetes.

Unfortunately, it's hard for a lot of people to take off 10 pounds. One approach has been suggested by psychologist Dr. John Foreyt, director of the Nutrition Research Center at Baylor College of Medicine in Houston and a well-known weight specialist. He recommends following what he calls the 250/250 rule: cut out 500 calories most days by reducing your food intake by 250 calories and increasing your physical activity level by 250. Since one pound generally equals 3,500 calories, you should lose a pound each week. The math doesn't always work out this neatly but after two and a half to three months you should be down 10 pounds.

Your weight-loss plan might be more enjoyable—maybe

even fun—if you share your experiences with another person. Your spouse, a friend, a co-worker, even someone you find on the Internet can help by cheering you on. In fact, research done by a Brown University graduate student found that on-line weight-loss groups are effective in helping people shed pounds.[10] In the study, a group of dieters who communicated via the Internet—they got advice from professionals about eating and exercise, and support from other dieters—dropped 9 pounds in twelve weeks. A control group who received only information off the Internet lost, on average, just 3 pounds in twelve weeks. Two popular programs, according to the *New York Times,* are the fee-based eDiets.com and the free Cyberdiet.com.

And don't give up. A study based on the National Weight Control Registry, a catalog of almost three thousand people who have maintained a weight loss of 30 pounds or more for one year or longer, found that these dieters usually tried many times before they succeeded.[11]

TAKING THE RIGHT VITAMINS

For generations, arthritis sufferers have searched for a dietary solution to their troubles. In the 1960s, some arthritis patients followed the "nightshade diet," eliminating tomatoes, egg-plants, bell peppers, and potatoes. Another diet of that same era forbade fruits, herbs, alcohol, dairy products, red meat, additives, and preservatives—which doesn't leave much in the refrigerator. These days, diets are less extreme. One current notion is that some people are allergic to certain foods and that allergic reactions precipitate arthritis symptoms. Removing the offending foods from the diet should thus alleviate the arthritis.[12]

This theory has little or no usefulness for osteoarthritis sufferers, however. What little evidence there is points to a connection between food allergies and rheumatoid arthritis, an autoimmune disease, but not OA. On the other hand, in recent years researchers have found one powerful connection between food and arthritis. Based on evidence from the Framingham Heart Study as well as other research, it appears that certain vitamins—D, C, and possibly E—may benefit people who already have osteoarthritis. Consuming appropriate amounts of these micronutrients will slow down the progress of osteoarthritis. It will not cure the illness or prevent it from starting, but it can buy time for those who already have it.

Vitamins C and E are antioxidants, which neutralize damaging free radicals (by-products of any oxidation process) and probably help protect the key cartilage components in the joints, the collagen, and the proteoglycans. Vitamin C is also important because its presence is required for the synthesis of the kind of collagen found in articular cartilage. In a subset of participants in the Framingham Heart Study, those with the highest intake of vitamin C had one-third less chance of severe progression of OA in the knee during a ten-year period than those with the lowest intake.[13] Vitamin C seemed to protect against cartilage loss. Vitamin E had a protective effect as well, but the data were less consistent.

A later analysis of the Framingham subjects looked at vitamin D, which is not an antioxidant.[14] Researchers found that a low to moderate intake of vitamin D created a threefold greater risk of progression of knee OA over ten years. Another study, done at the University of California at San Francisco, came up with similar results for osteoarthritis in the hip joint during an eight-year period.

Why would vitamin D matter? You may recall from Chapter 7 that some researchers consider OA a disease of the bones as much as a disorder of cartilage. As osteoarthritis progresses, the bones in the affected joints develop spurs and other abnormalities; in advanced cases, the bones may undergo stress fractures or tissue may die. Vitamin D is intimately bound up with the health of bones. Although bones seem solid, they are constantly adding and losing bone minerals, especially calcium, through a process known as remodeling. This procedure is set in motion by a complex network of hormones that includes an activated version of vitamin D. Getting an adequate amount of vitamin D—many people do not—may protect against some of the damage caused by osteoarthritis.

Thus, for people who already have OA, small changes can improve the prognosis. At a scientific conference on osteoarthritis sponsored by the National Institute of Arthritis and Musculoskeletal and Skin Diseases, Dr. Timothy E. McAlindon of Boston University, an investigator in the Framingham studies, said that simple dietary changes such as eating one or two servings of fruit a day (for vitamin C) and taking 400 international units (IU) of vitamin D (the RDA, or recommended daily allowance) might lower the risk of your OA worsening from high to medium.[15] One caveat on the vitamin D: stick to a pill that is no more than the 400 IU. Since D is fat-soluble, it remains in your body for some time and can build up to toxic levels if you take too much.

SHOULD YOU TAKE
GLUCOSAMINE SUPPLEMENTS?

Recently there has been a lot of press about glucosamine, an amino sugar produced in the body from glucose. Glucosamine is a building block for proteoglycans and also stimulates the synthesis of more proteoglycans, which is crucial for the health of cartilage inside a joint. Taking supplements is assumed to boost the repair of osteoarthritic cartilage. A number of European studies have attested to its efficacy, although at least one prominent American researcher insists that the benefits have been overstated. On the other hand, just recently a three-year-long Belgian study presented at the annual scientific meeting of the American College of Rheumatology showed, for the first time, that taking glucosamine sulfate supplements could prevent structural damage—narrowing of arthritic joints.[16] Several large-scale studies are now taking place in the United States that may corroborate these findings. In pills, glucosamine sulfate is often combined with chondroitin sulfate, a component of cartilage that helps proteoglycans hold on to water. The benefits of supplementation with this substance have not been well established, however.

SAM-e and glucosamine work in different ways, with SAM-e having a much broader range of action. The two ingredients are not incompatible. In fact, one nutraceutical company has the patent on a supplement that would combine SAM-e, glucosamine, and chondroitin sulfate, though it has not chosen to manufacture this product. Thus, if you really want to launch an all-out battle against arthritis, you can take both SAM-e and glucosamine. But if you want to take only one pill, SAM-e, an antidepressant that also improves liver health, gives a lot more bang for the buck.

Chapter 9

NEW HOPE FOR FIBROMYALGIA SUFFERERS

The mornings were always the hardest for Mary, who had suffered from fibromyalgia—debilitating muscle soreness and stiffness—for more than twenty years. "When I woke up I could barely move," says the forty-three-year-old freelance copy editor. As the day progressed, she continued to feel an overall tenderness, as if she had a flu that went on and on and on. "My neck and my back especially ached, and if you pressed hard anywhere it hurt," she recalls. The worst times were right before and during her period, when she also often got migraine headaches. And sleep provided little relief. "I have always had trouble getting to sleep and staying asleep," she says. Her energy level was so low that sometimes basic tasks, like shopping for groceries, seemed beyond her. Conventional jobs with regular business hours presented a problem, so Mary managed to make a not-so-great income working out of her home on her own schedule.

After years of visiting health care specialists, both conventional and alternative, Mary found some ways to deal with her fibromyalgia. To improve her sleep, she takes the kava, a mild herbal sedative, and melatonin, a naturally occurring hormone that reduces wakefulness. An elimination diet, in which she tested the impact of certain foods on her body by eating them and then stopping, found that she is allergic to citrus products;

when she stopped eating them she felt somewhat more ener-getic. Acupuncture also helped dull the pain, as did taking Advil (ibuprofen). Put together, all these measures made most of her days tolerable—but still difficult.

Then a friend suggested taking SAM-e. Mary began by swallowing one pill in the morning and one in the afternoon. The afternoon dose, she felt, made it harder to get to sleep so she switched to taking two in the morning. After four weeks, she increased the dosage to three pills (600 mg). Her first inkling that something was happening occurred when she went through a premenstrual week without having a migraine. Then, after eight weeks on SAM-e, she woke up one morning—and didn't ache. The next morning she had the same experience. It took a few more days for Mary to realize that she felt different. "My pain has gone from about a nine to a three. An enormous burden has been lifted off me," she says. Although she still needs her herbal medicine to sleep well, Mary now has enough energy to take a long walk every day and, more important, to get out and socialize. "I'm having fun, often, for the first time in a long, long while," she says.

WHAT IS FIBROMYALGIA?

Fibromyalgia is relentless, like a life sentence of hard labor with little chance of appeal. Little-understood and difficult to treat, the condition involves widespread flu-like pain in the soft tissues—muscles, tendons, ligaments—that lasts for over three months. The pain is not due to an underlying inflammatory or degenerative musculoskeletal disorder. Sufferers—an esti-mated 6 million in America, mostly women between age twenty and age fifty—also often feel stiff. Pain may never go away completely, although it may get better as the day goes on and may wax and wane over periods of several months. The diagnosis of fibromyalgia syndrome (FMS) is made if the sufferer has at least eleven out of eighteen possible tender points—areas that hurt when touched. These spots are mostly around the neck and the upper and lower back, but they can also appear near the knees, elbows, and hips.

People with fibromyalgia are often exhausted by their condition. They may operate in such a low gear that they have trouble keeping a job. Mary, for instance, lost her job with a book publisher when she was in her thirties because she called in sick so often that her employer regarded her as a malingerer. Another "fibro" patient, Sharon, survived on disability payments for two years before her symptoms abated enough for her to return to work. In various studies, some 10 to 30 percent of patients describe themselves as being work-impaired by FMS.

Fibromyalgia sufferers usually have myriad other symptoms and conditions, including migraine or tension headaches, irritable bowel syndrome (alternating diarrhea and constipation), painful menstrual periods, poor concentration, lack of focus (sometimes called brain fog), temporomandibular joint dysfunction syndrome (pain in the jaw and face, from clenching the jaw or from a malfunction of the jaw joint), food and chemical allergies, and dry mouth.

Most common of all is a sleep disorder called alpha-EEG anomaly. Fibromyalgia patients show abnormal brain waves during the deepest stage of sleep, stage four. Stage four sleep is important for the repair of tissues, the creation of antibodies, and the formation of growth hormone, which is necessary for muscle and bone health. Instead of experiencing the restorative rest that allows muscles to recover from a day of activity, fibro sufferers half-wake up during stage four sleep. If you've ever gone through a period of prolonged sleep deprivation, you know how achy you can end up being, and this is similar to how FMS sufferers feel. In fact, this lack of restful sleep is considered a major cause of the symptoms associated with FMS.

Fibro patients differ from the norm in other ways. Scientists have found that in their spinal fluid they have two to three times as much of a neurotransmitter called substance P, which relays chemical messages about pain. The overabundance of this chemical messenger may make FMS sufferers experience pain under circumstances that would not be uncomfortable to other people. At the same time, fibro patients also have low levels of growth hormone, which is needed for muscle repair, and of cortisol, a hormone produced by the adrenal gland that's associated with activating the body. People who are short on cortisol because of problems with their adrenal glands experience the same symptoms as FMS sufferers, according to recent studies by the National Institute of Arthritis and Musculoskeletal and Skin Diseases, an arm of the National Institutes of Health. Because of the chemical anomalies in fibro sufferers, the condition is sometimes called a neuroendocrine (neurological and hormonal) disease.

Many possible triggering events or causes have been blamed for the onset of FMS, including viral and bacterial infections, trauma such as an assault or auto accident, chemical and food sensitivities, immune response to breast implants, and quirks in muscle metabolism. Not one of these theories has been proven, though, and it is likely that people can get the symptoms of FMS in a variety of ways. "There are probably lots of different underlying problems," says Dr. Brian M. Berman, director of the complementary medicine program at the University of Maryland School of Medicine.

Just don't let anyone tell you that it's all in your head. While depression can accompany the chronic fatigue and pain of FMS—not a surprise, really—no one has ever shown that down moods cause the trouble.

CONVENTIONAL TREATMENTS: NOT VERY USEFUL

One of the greatest challenges facing FMS sufferers is finding a doctor who will take their symptoms seriously. "My family doctor told me I was stressed," says Sharon. "When I finally convinced him I needed medicine, he prescribed muscle relaxers that put me to sleep, which was not what I had in mind. I went to another doctor, who said I was depressed and tried to give me antidepressants. Again, not what I was looking for. Finally I visited a masseuse, who told me I probably had FMS and suggested I see a rheumatologist. I simply called up the biggest hospital and asked to see the head of the rheumatology department. He confirmed the diagnosis and began treating me."

Like Sharon, many people do not receive compassionate treatment until they find a rheumatologist, a doctor who specializes in joint, muscle, and bone disorders. Other types of physicians may also be helpful: physiatrists, who focus on muscles; osteopaths, who are trained to manipulate the spine; neurologists, who are experts on nerve diseases; pain specialists; M.D.'s with an interest in alternative medicine, and exceptional primary care physicians. Keep trying—even at university hospitals, it is perfectly possible to encounter physicians who deny the existence of fibromyalgia. For referral to a doctor near you who is knowledgeable about the condition, contact the Fibromyalgia Network at 800-853-2929, or www.fmnetnews.com. The Fibromyalgia Network also puts out an extremely informative newsletter.

Even after a fibro sufferer finds a sympathetic health care provider, however, she is not likely to experience a complete recovery. A study of FMS patients with symptoms severe enough to seek treatment from specialized centers showed that their condition changed little over seven years.[1] This means that they neither improved nor deteriorated. A study done in Australia of patients with milder cases was more hopeful: one-quarter of the patients were in remission two years after diagnosis.

Standard treatment for fibromyalgia focuses first on inducing the deep stage four sleep that allows for the renewal of muscles. Antidepressants, in smaller doses than are used to treat depression, may improve sleep, theoretically because they increase the availability of neurotransmitters like serotonin and norepinephrine. A common drug used is the tricyclic Elavil (amitriptyline), which is famous for its pain-relieving properties and ability to induce sleep. Because the drug can cause a foggy hangover the next morning, the recommendation is to take Elavil early in the evening, or to swallow a half-dose in the morning and the second half at bedtime.

Even in small doses, tricyclics like Elavil have powerful side effects such as dry mouth, constipation, and drowsiness, which many people cannot tolerate. And the medicine may not even work—only 30 to 50 percent of FMS patients experience substantial improvement. "The decrease in pain with these medications [tricyclics] has been significant but modest and tends to wane over time," writes Dr. Don L. Goldenberg, a rheumatologist at Tufts University School of Medicine, in a recent review article for the *Archives of Internal Medicine*.[2] A two-step treatment—Prozac in the morning and Elavil at night—has been shown to be somewhat more effective than either alone and may produce fewer side effects, since Prozac is a less toxic drug. However, many fibro people do not like the idea of spending their lives taking powerful drugs.

Many instead self-medicate with over-the-counter medicines like aspirin, Tylenol (acetaminophen), and especially Advil or other nonsteroidal anti-inflammatory drugs (NSAIDs), all of which have side effects, generally gastrointestinal, and none of which have been shown to work well. In bad flare-ups, doctors may resort to more serious measures such as a muscle relaxer like Flexeril (cyclobenzaprine) or injections at trigger points (centers of muscle spasms) with lidocaine or another synthetic version of the anti-inflammatory hormone cortisone. These shots often produce dramatic but short-lived relief as well as unpleasant side effects such as weight gain and thinning bones and skin.

For fibro sufferers, SAM-e might well be an improvement over conventional treatments.

HOW SAM-e CAN SOOTHE SORE MUSCLES

There are several reasons to believe that SAM-e may relieve some of the suffering of fibromyalgia syndrome. This naturally occurring supplement alters the balance of neurotransmitters like serotonin and norepinephrine in the brain—chemicals that may be associated with the experience of pain and poor sleep. In addition, SAM-e has known painkilling and anti-inflammatory properties. And since SAM-e produces almost no side effects, it is a big improvement over medications like anti-depressants and NSAIDs.

Yet, as a treatment for fibromyalgia, SAM-e is promising rather than proven. To date, three small studies of the connection have been published in English.[3] In the best study, done in 1991 by Danish rheumatology researchers, forty-four subjects with a diagnosis of fibromyalgia were given a daily oral dose of 800 mg of SAM-e or a placebo. After six weeks, the SAM-e group showed less pain, fatigue, and morning stiffness than the other patients, although there was not a drop in the number of tender points. An earlier study of seventeen patients in Italy, which used a less stringent definition of fibromyalgia, did find a drop in tender points after injection with SAM-e for twenty-one days. But the most recent study, by the earlier group of Danish researchers, found no significant improvement on SAM-e for thirty-four subjects. However, for reasons that are not clear, the study period only ran for ten days and, like the Italian study, used injections rather than oral doses of the drug.

The results of the studies indicate that much more research

is needed before a definitive answer is made about the usefulness of SAM-e for fibromyalgia. If the U.S. government won't fund this research—it has not so far—then the companies that manufacture SAM-e should take it upon themselves to test this application of the natural supplement. Fibro patients do not have a lot of good options, and any means of improving their well-being warrants a thorough investigation.

In the meantime, if you are suffering from fibromyalgia, it is worth trying SAM-e, which is a very safe supplement. Although you can't prove the effectiveness of a treatment on the basis of testimonials alone, it does appear that people with fibromyalgia have been helped by SAM-e. Sharon, who was quoted earlier, was able to work for the first time in two years after she began taking SAM-e. And Mary, the book editor, found significant relief from the supplement.

Both Sharon and Mary took fairly small doses of the supplement—either three or four pills a day. Since SAM-e is mildly energizing, anyone who suffers from insomnia—not uncommon in FMS patients—should swallow all the pills in the morning rather than divvying up the dose between morning and night.

There are additional ways FMS patients can improve their condition without resorting to powerful medicine.

OTHER WAYS OF COPING WITH FMS

The most effective way of coping with fibromyalgia, according to current thinking, is to combine a wide variety of approaches, both medical and nonmedical. In a recent review of nontraditional approaches, Dr. Brian Berman, of the University of Maryland School of Medicine, concluded that various mind-body techniques have shown the greatest success so far at improving the symptoms of fibromyalgia.[4] These techniques tap into the healing effect of the mind on the body. "In our programs," Dr. Berman says, "we teach people to do chi gung [or qi gong, a Chinese energy-balancing technique that's related to tai chi], breathing techniques, and visualization. These are very helpful." Other possibilities are biofeedback, hypnotherapy, meditation, and other relaxation techniques.

Along a similar vein, in his newsletter natural-healing guru Dr. Andrew Weil heartily recommends that fibromyalgia sufferers try out the Feldenkrais Method, a very gentle movement therapy.[5] Formulated by an Israeli scientist named Moishe Feldenkrais, this technique aims to reeducate your body so that you move with ease. It helps fibromyalgia sufferers change movement patterns that they have developed to avoid chronic pain but that may be increasing their daily discomfort.

The Web site for the Feldenkrais Guild (www.feldenkrais.com) provides some sample exercises, many geared toward people who work at computers. The Feldenkrais Guild keeps tight control over who can practice, and so the approximately 1,500 practitioners in the United States are likely to be competent. To find one, call the guild at 800-775-2118, or access its Web site.

Exercise is a common recommendation for fibromyalgia sufferers, though it is hard to do when you are stiff and in pain. It is best to start gradually, at even ten minutes a day, and slowly work up to twenty to thirty minutes four times a week. Focus on less physically stressful movement like water aerobics, swimming, stationary biking, elliptical trainers (nonimpact machines found in health clubs), and gentle yoga. Fast walking is easy to fit in to your schedule. Start by walking five minutes in one direction from your home, then turn around and go back. You'll barely notice that you are exercising. Then gradually increase your time.

Acupuncture, which involves stimulating points in the body to distribute *chi,* or energy, may relieve pain and improve functioning, although the data are not strong and some patients find it makes their symptoms worse.

Massage can also be double-edged. Deeper massage like Shiatsu and the especially intense Rolfing technique may not make you feel better. And even garden-variety massage therapists can cause soreness if they do not understand your condition. "I once left a massage session feeling as if I'd been battered with a two-by-four. Now I'm always clear ahead of time about where my sore spots are," says Mary. Relief often lasts for only a few hours, so massage may not be worth the high price tag—generally $35 to $100 an hour.

Finally, support groups, either on-line or in person, can boost the morale of a fibro patient. FMS sufferers often pretend they are feeling well so that they won't come off as complainers to their family and friends, but they are free to tell the truth among those who are similarly afflicted. Fellow sufferers can also exchange useful tips. People with fibromyalgia seem to be unusually sociable, and an enormous number of chat groups and e-mail discussion lists are available on the Web (use a search engine like Yahoo to find one you like). Doctors and clinics that specialize in FMS can provide references for face-to-face groups, or try ImmuneSupport.com, which has an on-line listing. Remember: A combination of techniques is most likely to yield relief. And SAM-e, since it presents virtually no side effects, is a safe bet.

Chapter 10

SAM-e FOR LIVER DISORDERS, AND OTHER PROMISING RESEARCH

The typical American becomes enthusiastic about SAM-e because it can alleviate the distress of depression and osteo-arthritis. But in scientific circles, the greatest buzz is about SAM-e's potential for treating liver damage, especially that caused by alcohol and viral infections like hepatitis. Even the U.S. government, which has generally paid little attention to this foreign-born supplement, has expressed interest in funding basic science research on the functions of S-adenosyl-methionine inside the liver.

One reason is that there is a dearth of effective treatments for liver diseases. Cirrhosis, in which the liver is irreversibly scarred, is the eighth leading cause of death in this country, and the fourth among middle-aged Americans. Current medical practice focuses mostly on reducing symptoms such as fluid retention, rectifying nutritional deficiencies through supple-mentation, and ending the patient's liquor consumption. In extreme cases, a liver transplant may be necessary.

You can see why any additional option would be welcome news. "SAM-e is going to become one of the treatments of choice for cirrhosis," says Dr. Charles Lieber, professor of medicine and pathology at Mount Sinai School of Medicine in New York City and director of the Alcohol Research and Treatment Center of the Bronx Veterans Affairs Medical

Center. "By itself SAM-e won't be the answer, but it will be part of a cocktail of drugs that will also include anti-inflammatories, antifibrotics, and antiviral medications, if needed," says Dr. Lieber.

The liver produces and utilizes most of the body's cache of S-adenosylmethionine, so it is natural that researchers would study its impact on the organ. But to understand how SAM-e could help liver disease, it is necessary to know a bit about how the organ operates.

THE BODY'S CHEMICAL PROCESSING PLANT

One of the biggest organs in the body, the liver performs a myriad of functions, which fall mostly within two job descriptions. As a filter, the liver detoxifies substances that get into the body via the digestive system (food, drinks, and drugs), by breathing (such as paint fumes), or through the skin (like certain medicines). As a regulator, it maintains the flow of fuel throughout the body by storing or altering macronutrients, including glucose (from carbohydrates), fats, and proteins, as well as micronutrients like vitamins A, B_{12}, D, E, K, and the minerals iron and copper. *Bile,* the best-known product of the liver, is crucial to both sets of functions. It helps remove toxins by surrounding them with a protective barrier until they are eliminated from the body in feces. Bile secreted from the liver, then stored in the gall bladder, also helps break down fatty foods (including fat-soluble vitamins) in the small intestine.

SAM-e contributes to the smooth operation of the liver in several ways. As a sulfur "donor," SAM-e is necessary for the manufacture of glutathione and taurine. Glutathione is a powerful antioxidant that is an essential player in the liver's detox-ification processes; taurine is a fat emulsifier. Both substances are important ingredients of bile salts, which in turn become the crucial liquid known as bile. Adequate levels of SAM-e are also necessary for the maintenance of liver cell membranes, DNA, and mitochondria (the cell's energy factory).

The power of SAM-e is demonstrated by its use as a detox-ifier in cases of lead poisoning. Studies in the 1980s on chronic lead poisoning in humans and mice showed that both oral and intravenous doses of SAM-e quickly cleared the toxin out of subjects' bloodstreams; much of the lead left the body through the feces.[1] The researchers believed that SAM-e's benefits come from its positive impact on the availability of glutathione. More recently, the Maryland company Nutramax has marketed SAM-e to veterinarians as a treatment for, among other things, drug overdoses (mostly acetaminophen, better known as Tylenol) in dogs and cats.

Additionally, in clinical studies SAM-e has been success-fully used to treat a condition in which a high amount of estro-gen, induced by pregnancy, impairs the flow of bile in some extremely sensitive women (known as intrahepatic cholestasis of pregnancy).[2] In the most recent study, done in 1998, the effectiveness of SAM-e improved when another medication, called ursodeoxycholic acid, was also used.

CIRRHOSIS OF THE LIVER: PERMANENT DAMAGE

In the United States, most cirrhosis is due to long-term, exces-sive alcohol intake, although chronic viral infections of the hepatic (liver) tissues, most often hepatitis C, also take a big toll. In small doses the liver handles alcohol well, but in large amounts its breakdown product, the potent free radical acetaldehyde, produces enormous damage. Excess acetalde-hyde reduces the liver's ability to release fat (in the form of fatty acids) into the body. These substances build up in the organ, causing an enlarged, or fatty, liver. Fatty liver is a reversible condition, but continued drinking or other assaults on the organ can lead to the formation of scar tissue, which interferes with the flow of bile and blood as well as other func-tions. Ultimately, someone who suffers from a cirrhotic liver risks becoming poisoned by his or her own toxins, which are no longer efficiently removed from the body. About 20 percent of people with cirrhosis also develop liver cancer.

How much liquor is dangerous for the liver? "It is possible for women to experience problems after drinking one and a half to two drinks a day for several years and, for men, three to four drinks a day," says Dr. Lieber. Individual susceptibility to liver disease is quite variable: in autopsies, an estimated 10 to 15 percent of alcoholics show evidence of cirrhosis, which means that 85 to 90 percent don't. Women are more vulnerable than men, in part because many have lower amounts of a stomach enzyme that breaks alcohol down into by-products that are less toxic to the liver.[3] Among both sexes, research suggests that there is a strong genetic basis for susceptibility to liver damage from alcohol consumption.[4]

Combining alcohol and acetaminophen is particularly treacherous for the liver, which is why labels on the over-the-counter drugs warn against taking the pills when consuming more than three alcoholic drinks in a day. The risk is not just in the long term, either. "You can get damage acutely and die from it," says Dr. Lieber. A lethal combination would consist of excessive amounts of each. Another highly dangerous situation occurs when someone who has hepatitis C drinks any alcohol.

Whatever the cause of the damage, a highly diseased liver can no longer regenerate itself. Normally, if you lose up to 80 percent of your liver, the remaining portion will enlarge so as to take up the empty space until the organ regains its original weight, a process that generally takes only a few months. This phenomenon makes it possible for people to donate portions of their livers to others without putting their own health in danger. In scarred cirrhotic livers, however, this renewal process cannot occur.

THE SAM-e SHORTAGE

Among people who suffer from cirrhosis, SAM-e is in short supply, and the reason appears to be the inhibition of an enzyme (S-adenosylmethionine synthetase) that allows methionine to combine with ATP to produce SAM-e.[5] The paucity of SAM-e causes several problems, including an excess of methionine, which is toxic for the liver in high doses; a shortage of the antioxidant glutathione; and a failure to produce a sufficient amount of bile. Studies with animals, including baboons, showed that SAM-e treatment could protect against the development of cirrhosis.[6]

But does remedying a SAM-e shortfall through supplementation improve liver functioning in people with cirrhosis? The answer is a guarded yes. Some short-term studies (thirty to sixty days) done in Italy during the 1970s found that the administration of SAM-e improves biological markers for cirrhosis. But only one study so far has followed the long-term outcome of cirrhosis patients given SAM-e.[7] For two years, this study, which appeared in a 1999 issue of the *Journal of Hepatology,* tracked the experiences of 123 patients with alcoholic cirrhosis, about half of whom received SAM-e (in an oral dose of 1,200 mg a day) and half received a placebo. When the most severely diseased patients were removed from the calculations, the overall liver transplantation and mortality rate was significantly higher in the placebo group (29 percent) than in the SAM-e group (12 percent). Lead author Dr. José Maria Mato, director of the Biochemistry and Cell Biology Laboratory in the Hepatology and Gene Therapy Program of the University of Navarra in Pamplona, Spain, states, "Our published results show that [SAM-e] treatment increases survival in patients with alcoholic liver cirrhosis, especially for those with less advanced disease." Says Dr. Lieber, "This impressive clinical study is a significant event."

In the year 2000, Dr. Mato will begin a second, confirmatory study. "The objective," he says, "is to treat, with the same dose of [SAM-e] that was used in the previous study (1,200 mg oral daily), around 300 patients with early-stage alcoholic liver cirrhosis for two years. We want to include in this trial a group of patients with alcoholic liver cirrhosis plus hepatitis C infection, and determine whether in this condition, which has a bad prognosis, [SAM-e] is also effective."

The unanswered question is whether or not taking SAM-e

can protect a relatively healthy person from developing liver problems. "The prophylactic use of S-adenosylmethionine has not been studied in clinical trials," says Dr. Lieber. However, in parts of Europe—where an obsession with the liver is often equivalent to Americans' fixation on the heart—SAM-e is routinely taken for what is seen as minor liver dysfunction. Writes Dr. Steven Bratman, medical director of the Natural Pharmacy (TNP.com), an on-line service, "SAM-e is also used in Europe as a treatment for 'minor hepatic insufficiency,' a syndrome not recognized in U.S. medical circles. In this condition, the liver is supposed to be functioning somewhat below par, even though there are no measurable changes in liver enzymes.... Symptoms are said to include fatigue, general malaise, digestive disturbances, allergies, PMS, and constipation."[8]

So far, this diagnosis has not caught on in America. Nor is any expert suggesting that healthy people take SAM-e to prevent liver problems—yet.

RESEARCH ON PARKINSON'S DISEASE AND ALZHEIMER'S DISEASE

Actor Michael J. Fox, Attorney General Janet Reno, and three-time heavyweight champion Muhammad Ali all suffer from Parkinson's disease, a progressive disorder of the central nervous system that was first described in England in 1817 by Dr. James Parkinson, who called it shaking palsy. The telltale signs are muscle rigidity (stiffness), difficulty beginning and ending movements (such as walking), tremors (uncontrollable motions, especially in the hands), loss of balance, and muscle aches. About 40 percent of people with Parkinson's also suffer from depression. Parkinson's disease afflicts about one million Americans, most of them over the age of fifty.

The disorder is caused by an increasing deterioration of nerve cells in the substantia nigra, the area of the brain that manufactures dopamine, a neurotransmitter which, among other things, is crucial to muscle movement. People who suffer from Parkinson's are known to experience a shortage of dopamine; this paucity also wrecks the balance in the body between dopamine and other neurotransmitters like acetycholine. The standard treatment for Parkinson's disease increases the amount of available dopamine by providing an amino acid that is the precursor for the neurotransmitter. This is manufactured as the drug levodopa, or L-dopa. The substance reduces the symptoms of Parkinson's disease but does not slow down its progression. A medication called carbidopa is often used in conjunction with L-dopa to reduce side effects and slow its breakdown.

Since SAM-e is known to influence dopamine and acetylcholine levels, it seems like a reasonable treatment for Parkinson's disease, or at least for the depression that often accompanies the ailment. In his book, *Stop Depression Now* (Putnam, 1999), Columbia University's Dr. Richard Brown recounts a successful trial he co-conducted in which taking SAM-e substantially improved the mood of Parkinson's sufferers. He also reports using the nutraceutical successfully to treat the tremors of his patients with Parkinson's disease. Since these results have not yet been replicated in a scientific manner, however, they can only be considered exploratory. If you are afflicted with Parkinson's, discuss the use of SAM-e with your doctor thoroughly before taking it.

The evidence on SAM-e and Alzheimer's disease is somewhat more promising.

An estimated 2.5 to 4 million Americans, including former President Ronald Reagan, suffer from the dementia known as Alzheimer's, named after Alois Alzheimer, the German neurologist who first reported it. This troubling and perplexing ailment brings about the progressive deterioration of a sufferer's memory, intellect, and, later, motor abilities. In the latest stages, Alzheimer's sufferers may be unable to carry on a conversation, feed themselves, or respond to other people. MRIs, CTs, and X-rays show an atrophy (shrinking) in the frontal or temporal lobes of the brain. The precise cause of Alzheimer's is unknown, but different factors are being investigated, including genetic traits (about 5 to 10 percent of cases appear to be inherited), slow viruses, exposure to metals such as aluminum, and biochemical abnormalities such as alterations in the level of acetycholine in the brain.

One Canadian study has found that levels of SAM-e are severely decreased in the brains of people with Alzheimer's, and some very tentative research suggests that the nutraceutical can improve the cognitive functioning of some sufferers.[9] The presumed mechanism would be SAM-e's ability to increase the availability of neurotransmitters, including acetycholine. Unfortunately, because so little is known about Alzheimer's, those concerned about the disease may have a long wait before definitive results about the usefulness of SAM-e appear.

OTHER DISORDERS

Research with SAM-e has also been done on other disorders. Some small studies have suggested that SAM-e may be useful for treating migraine headaches, withdrawal symptoms from opiates, and attention deficit disorder.[10] Although promising, none of these findings have yet been confirmed in large studies.

CAN SAM-e SLOW DOWN THE AGING PROCESS?

While most manufacturers present SAM-e as a treatment for depression, arthritis, and fibromyalgia, a certain segment of the natural supplement market is touting this nutraceutical as an antiaging pill. This would mean that the pill brakes, or possibly even reverses, some of the changes that happen when people grow older. For many persons, these changes are not very appealing.

As we age, our systems slow down. Our immune systems become less efficient at protecting our bodies. Our nerve and muscle cells respond to our commands a bit less quickly. After the age of forty, it begins to seem impossible to lose extra weight. The infectious diseases that are so prevalent among children give way to chronic ailments like heart disease, diabetes, osteoarthritis, and cancer. While there are many theories of aging—and they are not necessarily mutually exclusive—one important hypothesis attributes signs of aging to an accumulation of genetic mistakes made as cells divide—that is, a lifetime's worth of DNA errors, some more consequential than others.

Because SAM-e appears in higher concentrations in young

people, and then declines as we get older, some researchers assume that it is biologically associated with youthfulness.[11] And SAM-e does appear to have certain antiaging properties. Methylation, a major biochemical pathway that calls for SAM-e, helps prevent cell mutations and plays a role in turning genes on and off. The presence of SAM-e is also crucial for the production of a powerful antioxidant known as glutathione, which allows the liver to detoxify the body and helps joints successfully renew themselves, thus slowing down the development of osteoarthritis. SAM-e is also essential for the building of lipid-fat phospholipids, fats that make cell membranes supple and allow nutrients and other substances to pass in and out easily.[12] This permeability may keep cells "youthful."

SAM-e may also help keep blood vessels flowing smoothly. S-adenosylmethionine is intricately connected to homocysteine, a by-product of the methylation process (after SAM-e "donates" a methyl group, it breaks down to form homocysteine). This destructive substance appears to create the initial damage associated with atherosclerosis, or hardening of the arteries. Homocysteine scars the cells that line the arteries, setting the stage for later deposits of cholesterol, which narrow the blood vessels. These impaired arteries, in turn, allow for the blood clots that cause strokes and the stoppage of blood flow that results in heart attacks. Close to eighty studies have found an association between high homocysteine levels in the blood and hardening or blockage of arteries.

Taking B vitamins may reduce the amount of homocysteine in your bloodstream. Swallowing SAM-e may do so, too, according to Dr. Teodoro Bottiglieri. There are two pathways through which homocysteine can be neutralized. One way is for it to become remethylated back to SAM-e, which requires the presence of folic acid (a B vitamin) and vitamin B_{12}. Some homocysteine, in addition, becomes transformed into the precursor of glutathione, the powerful antioxidant. This process can only happen when SAM-e and vitamin B_6 are available. Thus a shortage of SAM-e could lead to a surplus of homocysteine.

There is yet another way in which SAM-e might help hold back the clock. In the United States there is a strong connection between feeling young and feeling energetic. Thus, people who take SAM-e and become more energetic may well seem younger to both themselves and others.

Do these benefits mean that SAM-e is a veritable fountain of youth? Hardly. But they do say that you are doing your body a lot of good if you are taking SAM-e for depression, arthritis, or fibromyalgia. But if the only reason you're interested in SAM-e is to stave off aging, you have simpler and less expensive options, such as exercising regularly, eating lots of fruits and vegetables, and giving up smoking.

Chapter 11

HOW TO TAKE SAM-e

For many people, the chance to relieve discomfort without having to deal with a doctor is part of SAM-e's draw. Yet throughout this book you have been advised to consult with your doctor before taking SAM-e, especially in larger doses. Is this realistic? Is the physician who gives you flu shots and prescribes antibiotics for your sore throats really going to offer any help on something that's considered alternative medicine?

There are really two issues here. One is whether your regular M.D. will look down on you, or brush away your ideas, if you bring up the possibility of trying SAM-e, a nonconventional medicine. The second is whether your doctor is well enough informed about SAM-e to serve up reasonable advice.

On the first count, it is not clear how many American doctors now dismiss complementary medical treatments out of hand. A 1993 study in the *New England Journal of Medicine* reported that 34 percent of Americans make use of alternative medicine (very broadly defined), and that only 40 percent of alternative therapies were disclosed to doctors.[1] A follow-up study by the same set of researchers, published in 1998, determined that the percentage of Americans turning to alternative medicine had increased to 42 percent, yet the disclosure rate remained unchanged.[2]

These figures have been widely reported and discussed in

the medical literature; many physicians consider the conceal-
ment of information by their patients a significant problem. In
other words, while many M.D.'s might wish that their patients
would not use alternative medicines, they would still rather
know about them than not know.

RELYING ON A PHYSICIAN

Clearly many Americans try to avoid censure by their physicians. Yet the potential scorn is worth the risk, because your
doctor can make sure that your symptoms are not caused by a
problem you would not know about. For instance, depression
can be a side effect of hypothyroidism, or an underactive thyroid, and might disappear quickly when the underlying condition is treated. In addition, it is helpful for your future care that
your doctor maintain records of the supplements you take.
While SAM-e is not known to produce any negative interactions with drugs and supplements, it is possible more information will arise. Right now it is understood, for example, that the
vitamin B_6 you are recommended to take in conjunction with
the nutraceutical can offset the benefits of L-dopa, which is
used to treat Parkinson's disease.

It is hard to know in advance if your doctor will be familiar
with SAM-e. Rheumatologists, who treat people suffering from
arthritis and fibromyalgia, appear to be unusually knowledgeable about alternative treatments, probably because conventional medicine often fails their patients. One study found that
62 percent of patients who told their rheumatologists about
their use of complementary medicine got either a positive or
a neutral response. In addition, a surprising number of psychi-

atrists appear to be aware of SAM-e. In 1999, when the American Psychiatric Association invited Dr. Richard Brown to speak at a symposium during its annual meeting, he drew a standing-room-only crowd. Ten years earlier, when Dr. Bruce Kagan addressed the same meeting about SAM-e, the audience consisted of "the three presenters and our families," he says, only half joking.

One can assume that the knowledge of SAM-e will spread among physicians, especially those who specialize in arthritis and depression, as news of its good results becomes known.

In the meantime you can often get your questions answered by your local pharmacist, particularly if SAM-e is sold in the store. One caveat: Don't take advice from a health food or vitamin store employee. No matter how well-meaning they are, they are not trained to provide information important to your health. Relying on them for recommendations would be like hiring a hitchhiker to rebuild the engine of your Porsche.

TRYING THE ALTERNATIVE ROUTE

Osteopaths, who have as much training as medical doctors and who are similarly licensed by states to practice medicine, come out of a tradition that emphasizes spinal manipulation to ease problems. While some osteopaths are undistinguishable from M.D.'s, most are more favorable to alternative medicine than the typical medical school graduate. You can find one in your state by contacting this organization:

American Osteopathic Association
142 East Ontario Street

Chicago, Illinois 60611

800-621-1773

www.am-osteo-assn.org

If you want to consult a physician who's guaranteed to have an alternative-medicine bent, you can find one through the AHMA:

American Holistic Medical Association

6728 Old McLean Village Drive

McLean, VA 22101

703-556-9728

www.holisticmedicine.org

In addition, you can opt for a naturopathic physician, who is a health practitioner but does not have the advanced training of an M.D. or osteopath. In the nineteen states (plus Puerto Rico) where they are licensed, naturopathic physicians (N.D.'s) function like the alternative-medicine version of family practitioners. Trained in specialized colleges, and required to pass a national exam, they are generalists who emphasize diet and lifestyle, who prescribe botanical and over-the-counter medicines (and, in some states, simple medications like antibiotics), and who generally spend much more time with you than M.D.'s. Good naturopathic physicians maintain relationships with medical doctors to whom they refer cases that are beyond their expertise. You can locate an N.D. near you by contacting this organization:

American Association of Naturopathic Physicians

601 Valley, Suite 105

Seattle, WA 98109

206-298-0125

www.naturopathic.org

Be warned that many of these alternative-medicine practitioners lean toward botanical remedies, especially St. John's wort, an herbal that is not always effective. Psychiatrists, on the other hand, often dismiss St. John's wort. "You just don't know what's in it," says Dr. Bruce Kagan. Whereas SAM-e contains only one active chemical ingredient, St. John's wort contains an estimated fifty.

HOW MUCH SAM-e SHOULD YOU TAKE?

If you are treating yourself, it is hard to know how much SAM-e to take. The ideal dosage varies by condition and by the particular needs of the person using it. Every now and then you will come across a recommendation to start taking SAM-e at a high dose, presumably to flood your system, then go down to a lower one. This advice is counterintuitive: if you have any problems adjusting to SAM-e (say, it gives you loose bowels), your reactions will probably be more intense with higher doses. You would be better off taking a low dose, and experiencing a milder side effect, than bringing on a large side effect with a big dose.

Additionally, if you are unusually sensitive to medications—this is especially pertinent to people who suffer from fibromyalgia because they often have many allergies—start with only 200 mg, or one SAM-e pill, a day, then ratchet up the dosage accordingly.

For depression: Most studies on depression have relied on a dosage of 1,600 mg, or eight 200mg SAM-e pills, a day, which would require a substantial outlay of funds. Manufacturers most often recommend a much smaller amount, usually 400 mg, or two 200mg pills a day—still expensive but possible for many people. Experts have successfully treated people, especially those with mild to moderate depression, with a two-pill 400mg daily dose, or slightly higher, and this is how you should begin. SAM-e normally begins relieving depression within a few days; if your mood doesn't significantly get better after ten to fourteen days, move up to 800 mg (four pills) a day for another ten to fourteen days.

If you still don't see improvement, it's time to consult a medical professional, who may try SAM-e in combination with another drug or switch to a new regimen entirely. On your own, of course, you could gradually add pills until you see if the 1,600mg dose alters your mood. While this is perfectly safe physiologically, you would miss out on expert assistance in treating what could be a severe depression. If you are determined to medicate yourself without a doctor, pay close attention to how you are responding. To learn more about the experiences of ordinary users, go to a discussion group aimed at people who take SAM-e for depression: www.delphi.com/samesupport/messages. Compared to other depression discussion groups, by the way, this is quite a cheery crowd.

For osteoarthritis: Most research on SAM-e has used a 1,200mg or higher daily regimen, but one long-term study found significant improvement with a dosage of 400 mg a day for a two-year period. Start with 400 mg a day of SAM-e for two weeks. If you do not feel better, increase your intake to 800 mg a day for another two weeks. Discontinue SAM-e if your arthritic symptoms have not been reduced. One caveat: SAM-e does not work as quickly on osteoarthritis as it does on depression. You may need to take it for at least two weeks before you feel better.

For fibromyalgia: In the most rigorous study of fibromyalgia, subjects found relief with 800 mg of SAM-e a day. But it has worked for people at lower doses. As before, start with a dose of 400 mg a day for two weeks; then, if need be, move up to 800 mg a day. Should that dose not relieve your symptoms, you may assume that SAM-e is not working for you.

WHO SHOULD NOT TAKE SAM-e

If you have any personal or family history of manic-depression, if you experience panic attacks, or if you are pregnant or nursing, do not use SAM-e except under the direction of a physician.

WHEN TO TAKE SAM-e

Experts generally suggest taking SAM-e two times a day, with the first dose in the early morning and the second in the late morning or late afternoon. Afternoon pills can give you a lift that may help you through the daily energy low that occurs for almost all of us at around 4:00 or 5:00 P.M. But evening dosing is discouraged because, as an activating substance, SAM-e can cause insomnia. People who have trouble remembering to take pills can take them all at once in the morning without any ill effects, says Dr. Lewis Opler.

It is important to swallow SAM-e on a relatively empty stomach, because this dramatically improves absorption rates. In one study, plasma (blood) levels of SAM-e were 3.5 times higher for those who took it in the morning on an empty stomach as for those who took the pill after eating a meal. Consuming a snack or breakfast, however, should not interfere with the absorption, and might be necessary for those who get upset stomachs from the pills.

GETTING ENOUGH B VITAMINS

Morning is the easiest time to also take a vitamin B complex pill. Experts consistently suggest that you ensure you have adequate amounts of certain B vitamins in your system to make the best use of SAM-e. That's because two crucial chemical pathways that SAM-e boosts—methylation and transsulfuration—require the presence of vitamins B_6 and B_{12} as well as folic acid. You should know that this recommendation has never been directly tested; not one of the studies of SAM-e manipulated the supplementation of B vitamins. In Pharmavite's upcoming large-scale depression research project, discussed in Chapter 5, this issue will be addressed.

The theoretical reasons for taking B vitamins with SAM-e are strong, though, and many other health benefits accrue from this practice. Various B vitamins act as coenzymes in the body, which means that they help other enzymes jump-start chemical reactions. Folic acid, vitamin B_6, and vitamin B_{12} have been shown to lower artery-damaging homocysteine levels in the body, helping to protect against heart disease. Folic acid is so useful for protecting against several neural tube birth defects, including spina bifida, that the government in 1998 mandated that it be added to enriched flour, which ends up in the bread we eat. It also doubled the recommended daily allowance (RDA) of this micronutrient to 400 mcg a day.

Many Americans, especially women, fail to get enough of the B vitamins, particularly folic acid and B_6, from their diets. Vegetarians often fall short on vitamin B_{12}, since it comes mainly from animal sources like red meat. People who drink may deplete their bodies of vitamin B_1 (thiamine), and oral contraceptives are known to interfere with the absorption of folic acid, B_2 (riboflavin), B_6, and B_{12}. Since the various B vitamins tend to work in tandem, the usual recommendation is to take a B complex pill at 100 or 150 percent of the RDA of the micronutrients so as to ensure that they all operate efficiently. Another possibility is to cover all your bases by taking a daily multiple vitamin. Avoid megadosing, however. An excess of vitamin B_6 (at around 25 times the RDA), in particular, can temporarily harm the nerves in your arms and legs. Incidentally, vitamin B_2 in a pill may turn your urine bright yellow. It is nothing to worry about.

IF YOU MISS A DOSE

If you forget to take your morning pill(s), you can make up for it (or them) later in the day, but don't double up the next day if you've missed 24 hours' worth of SAM-e. Try not to make skipping pills a habit. When you treat chronic conditions like arthritis and depression, you need to keep the nutraceutical circulating in your body for optimal results.

POSSIBLE SIDE EFFECTS

SAM-e's major selling point is that, unlike conventional antidepressants and conventional arthritis treatments, it generally does not produce side effects. However, a few sensitive people may experience headaches, insomnia, or mild gastrointestinal distress (loose bowels, flatulence, upset stomach, heartburn), but these tend to go away within a few days. Thankfully quite rare are more serious side effects. In susceptible people, SAM-e can cause a switch from depression to mania. Also, like other antidepressants, it can spark a panic attack in people who are prone to have them.

STORING SAM-e

As a compound, SAM-e is chemically unstable. When exposed to moisture, it will take up water and quickly deteriorate. The packaging should prevent the product from being affected by normal household humidity. Thus it is fine to store your SAM-e in your bathroom cabinet. However, you risk seriously degrading the product and ruining its effectiveness if you keep it in the refrigerator.

Don't take the pills out of the container and place them elsewhere. They will degrade in the presence of humidity. A Harvard-affiliated study in the early 1990s came up with such strange results that some other American researchers lost interest in the subject of SAM-e. What happened: After the professors removed the pills from their double foil blister packs and put them in bottles, the pills deteriorated to the point where they lost their chemical potency.

If kept in the original container, stored SAM-e will generally remain effective for at least two years. As with any supplement, though, it is better to use it fresh. It is also crucial to buy products that really deliver, as we shall see in the next chapter.

Chapter 12

A SHOPPER'S GUIDE TO SAM-e

It sounds almost laughably obvious: A supplement should contain what it says on the label. But several studies have found that in the unregulated world of supplements, it's buyer beware. For instance, testing by the independent ConsumerLab.com found that one-quarter of thirty brands of ginkgo biloba (an herb that's purported to improve memory) did not contain the proper amount of the appropriate chemicals.[1] The company's study of saw palmetto products, which are used in the United States primarily to treat an enlarged prostate gland, found that only seventeen out of twenty-seven contained the active ingredients that were available in formulations used in clinical trials.

GETTING WHAT YOU PAY FOR

Defective merchandise is also a risk with SAM-e, which is especially problematic because it must be manufactured under climate-controlled conditions to prevent degradation. In an editorial entitled "Beware the Son of SAM-e," Al Czap, publisher of the *Alternative Medicine Review,* worried about what would happen as American companies, which have no experience manufacturing the nutraceutical, began packaging the raw material.[2] Only a few U.S. brands are licensed to carry the pharmaceutical grade product produced by the Italian company

Knoll SPa. "I am very disquieted," he wrote, "considering the consequences that might arise because of those U.S. dietary supplement manufacturers who...will simply capsule or tablet SAM-e on their own and heave it into the marketplace."

A sophisticated chemical analysis of eight brands by the Good Housekeeping Institute, an arm of the venerable magazine, showed that Czap was right to worry.[3] *Good Housekeeping* wrote: "What we found was shocking. In three brands we detected less active ingredient than listed in the bottle. In one brand we detected no active ingredient at all." To name names, the two brands in this test that ran at about half the stated value were Aspen and FoodScience of Vermont. The one with no detectable SAM-e was Nature's Vision (the manufacturer told the Good Housekeeping Institute that it is now using a more stable version of the nutraceutical than it was when the testing took place). As A1 Czap later put it during an interview, "There's a lot of useless material out there."

WHAT TO LOOK FOR: CHEMICAL STABILITY

With SAM-e, the big problem is preventing the chemical from breaking down when it is exposed to air and moisture. The stability of SAM-e is affected by its formulation. SAM-e comes in two types of salts, the older tosylate and the newer butane disulfonate. The older technique was the predominant one until recently, when Knoll SPa and its German parent company BASF patented another method of making SAM-e. In terms of stability, butane disulfonate has a slight edge over the older method. Most of the testing on SAM-e, however, was done when the product was still made in a tosylate formulation, and experts feel that the difference is small so long as the nutraceutical is manufactured under strictly controlled conditions.

Similarly, tablets sealed in a foil blister pack, which are opened one at a time, are slightly more stable than those in a bottle, which are exposed to air and moisture each time the container is opened. But again, it does not seem that the loss in stability is important if the pills are well made.

On the other hand, enteric coating is crucial to the usefulness of SAM-e. The coating, which helps protect SAM-e from moisture and air, also prevents the pills from being digested in the stomach but allows them to be broken down in the intestine. If the uncoated pills are exposed to stomach acids, they become chemically inert and are doing nothing for you. Avoid packages that do not explicitly say that the pills are enteric coated.

Another no-no is a liquid formulation. Unless it is in an ampule designed for a single injection, any fluid product will rapidly degrade.

A GUIDE TO DIFFERENT BRANDS

Here are most of the reputable brands of SAM-e currently available.

NATURE MADE: The gold standard, this butane disulfonate formulation is manufactured in Italy by Knoll SPa, the company that first produced SAM-e supplements. Good Housekeeping Institute's testing found 286 mg for pills labeled 200 mg, an excess that allows for some deterioration of the active ingredient. Enteric-coated 200mg pills are packed in foil blisters to keep them from being affected by humidity, and come in 20-

and 60-tablet packages. The box includes a handy informational insert. This product is easy to find at Web-based drugstores and is also sold at K mart and warehouse discounters like Costco. The best price is around $1.00 per 200mg pill, retail (on sale); the price can go down to $.75 on the Internet. For questions about use, phone 800-276-2878.

GNC (GENERAL NUTRITION CENTER): Also butane disulfonate, and also made by Knoll SPa in Italy, this brand comes in an opaque brown package and holds not one but two silica gel containers. Enteric-coated pills are available in 200mg and (oddly) 100mg sizes. GHI's testing came up with 147 mg for a 100mg pill. The best price per 200mg pill is $1.33. For more information on the product, call 888-462-2548.

NUTRALIFE: This is a tosylate formulation that comes in moisture-resistant foil-blister packs. The enteric-coated pills are available only on the Web, at www.nutralife.com. They are sold as one, six, or twelve boxes, with the price declining in larger quantities. The best price per 200mg pill is $1.10. Phone number: 877-688-7254.

SOLGAR: This well-known supplement manufacturer supplies a tosylate version of enteric-coated SAM-e (called SAM Sulfate) which is presented in a dark glass container. The label features unusual directions ("Take with a carbohydrate snack") that are probably generic to the company and are appropriate for vitamin pills but not SAM-e, which is absorbed much better when swallowed on an empty stomach. In GHI's testing, a

200mg pill contained 273 mg. The product sells, in a retail store, for about $2.71 per 200mg pill, but it costs much less on the VitaminShoppe.com Web site. For more information call 201-944-2311.

VITAMIN SHOPPE: This enteric-coated version of SAM-e is sold in an amber glass bottle. The ingredients list says that the pills are either tosylate or butane disulfonate, which is strange because Knoll SPa owns the patent on the latter formulation. The cost, retail, for a 200mg pill is $1.50; prices are lower on the VitaminShoppe.com site. Phone: 800-223-1216.

NATURE'S PLUS: Called Rx-Mood SAM-e, this Nature's Plus product is enteric-coated, tosylate, and sold in a twenty-tablet bottle. A 200mg pill, according to GHI's research, contains 216 mg. The cost, from a retail store, is $2.71 per 200mg pill (much less from VitaminShoppe.com). With questions, call 516-293-0030.

MOTHERNATURE: These enteric-coated tosylate pills are pack-aged in a white plastic container and are available in thirty- and sixty-tablet bottles. The product is sold only on the Internet, at www.mothernature.com. The lowest cost for a 200mg pill is $.87. For more information, call 800-517-9020.

LIFE EXTENSION: This company sells blister-packed SAM-e, which it claims is a butane disulfonate formulation, although Knoll SPa holds that patent. Boxes come in twenty- and fifty-pill sizes, and can be bought in bulk (eight twenty-tablet boxes, four fifty-tablet boxes). Sold on the Web site (www.lef.org) and by catalog. The best deal for a 200mg pill is $.96. Direct your questions to 877-900-9073.

SAVING MONEY

If you don't want to pay full retail price—who would?—your best alternatives are to shop at a warehouse discount store like Costco, to wait for sales in retail stores, or to shop from the Internet. If you can get a 200mg pill for less than a dollar, you are doing well.

GETTING BARGAINS ON THE WEB

The following information is current as of this writing. Bear in mind that Web sites may alter their addresses or just disappear one day. On-line drugstores frequently offer specials and change prices, so you should always comparison-shop before you order. The best bargain today may well not be the greatest deal tomorrow. Make sure you also factor in the cost of shipping. If you are not on the Internet, a couple of the following sites also have catalogs they can mail to you.

DrugStore.Com (www.drugstore.com): "A World of Products and the Expertise to Help You Find What You Need." You can purchase vitamins, supplements, beauty products, and prescription drugs on this site. A Wellness Guide provides information on drug interactions (only the top twenty medicines, though), treatments by condition, herbal remedies, and homeopathic products. The site also provides well-balanced information on supplements like SAM-e. DrugStore.com sells GNC brand SAM-e at the same prices the retail stores offer. Twenty Nature Made 200mg SAM-e tablets go for $18.99; sixty 200mg tablets cost $52.99. Return policy: Advises customers to contact the company via e-mail first to see if it is necessary to return the product for credit. Shipping: $3.49, within two to three days. Fast, reliable delivery is a big advantage with this company. Bonus point: Saturday delivery.

HealthQuick (www.healthquick.com): "Never, Never Undersold Drugstore." A bare-bones site that really does (as of this writing) provide the lowest-cost twenty-tablet box of SAM-e— $16.88 for Nature Made 200mg pills. A sixty-tablet box of the same product sells for $49.88. HealthQuick, whose site includes a small on-line library, offers vitamins, supplements, beauty items, and health care products. Return policy: Full refund if you notify the company of your dissatisfaction via e-mail. Shipping: $2.95 for under $20, free for $20 and up, within three to five business days.

ImmuneSupport.com (www.immunesupport.com): "Your Immune Support and Chronic Pain Specialist." The site is dedicated to those who suffer from chronic fatigue syndrome and fibromyalgia. There is a newsletter on these subjects, with access to archives, as well as information on support groups, legal issues (especially getting on disability), and new research. The company sells Nature Made 200mg SAM-e pills (twenty for $17.99; sixty for $48.99) as well as a SAM-e MaxPack that combines sixty Nature Made SAM-e pills with a separate bottle of one hundred Ultra-B Complex pills (with at least the

RDA of the B vitamins, plus PABA, choline, and inositol) for $59.92. You can return any unused pills for a refund. Shipping: $4.95 within three to seven business days. Bonus point: Discount shopper program with automated monthly shipment and 33 percent off the standard price. Note: You may need to enter this site through a search engine as the Web address does not always respond. For a catalog call 800-366-6056.

Life Extension Foundation (www.lef.org): "The World's Largest Organization Dedicated to Scientific Methods to Slow and Reverse Aging." The large site provides excerpts from the *Life Extension* magazine, discussion groups, links to medical journal abstracts, and new research findings. Members of this organization-with-an-agenda ($75 for the first year) receive deep discounts on its brand of supplements. If you are dissatisfied in any way, you can return your purchase and LEF will replace the product or credit your account. Shipping: $4.50 (delivery can be slow). Bonus point: An online "FDA Museum"—a high-tech bashing of the federal agency's misdeeds, tailor-made for people of a certain persuasion. To obtain a product catalog, phone 800-841-5433.

MotherNature.com (www.mothernature.com): "Natural Products. Healthy Advice." MotherNature.com sells not just supplements but also organic food, pet supplies, and beauty products. The company carries its own brand of SAM-e as well as Nature Made's. It offers a SAM-e multipack—four twenty-tablet boxes of Nature Made (200 mg)—for $80.97, or about $1 per pill. (One twenty-tablet box goes for $22.49; one sixty-tablet box costs $53.19.) An on-line health journal includes some stories from *Prevention* magazine, and the site posts several specially written articles about SAM-e. You can return the unused portion of your order within thirty days for a full refund. Shipping: $3.95 for orders under $50, free for $50 and over, within four to eight business days. Bonus point: One-time new-customer discount of 50 percent off, with a ceiling of $50.

PlanetRx.com (www.planetRx.com): "Life Is Better on Planet-Rx." As much an entertainment center as a shopping center, this site provides a community (live chats and message boards) along with products (prescription drugs, supplements, medical supplies, beauty products). Snappy little stories offer health updates. In addition, PlanetRx.com links to satellite sites (such as arthritis.com and depression.com) that give some information about disorders. A twenty-tablet pack of Nature Made SAM-e (200 mg) sells for $16.99; a sixty-tablet pack costs $52.79. You can return the product within thirty days for a full refund. Shipping: $3.95 within three to five days. Bonus point: Advice from pharmacists (on-line or by phone) is available twenty-four hours a day.

Vitamin Shoppe (www.vitaminshoppe.com): "Over 18,000 Products and 400 Brands." This site offers a large variety of SAM-e brands—six in all, including its own brand. At this writing, Vitamin Shoppe offers the lowest price for a sixty-tablet box of Nature Made 200mg SAM-e, $44.99; a twenty-tablet box goes for $17.99. (Vitamin Shoppe refers to Nature Made as Pharmavite, its parent company.) The site provides links to several important health sites, such as DrKoop.com and Ask Dr. Weil, as well as to its own vitaminbuzz.com, which offers encyclopedic information about drug interactions, diets and therapies, and herbal and homeopathic remedies. If you are dissatisfied with any product you can return the unused portion within thirty days for a credit. Shipping: $4.95, for next day air.

NOTES

CHAPTER ONE: HOW SAM-e CAN HELP YOU

1. The figures come from the Institute of Medicine of the National Academy of Medicine.
2. For a chilling account of the manipulation of statistics to achieve the approval of the antidepressant Serzone, see Thomas J. Moore, "Hard to Swallow," *Washingtonian,* Dec. 1997.
3. The expert is Dr. Robert Brook, head of the Rand Corporation's health studies program and a professor at the University of California, Los Angeles, Medical School, quoted in "Medicine Remains As Much Art As Science," *New York Times,* Sept. 21, 1997.

CHAPTER TWO: WHAT MAKES SAM-e WORK?

1. P. Giulidori et al., "Transmethylation, Transsulfuration, and Aminopropylation Reactions of S-adenosyl-L-methionine in Vivo," *Journal of Biological Chemistry,* 259, no. 7 (Apr. 10, 1984), 4205–11.

CHAPTER THREE: THE BIRTH OF THE BLUES

1. T. G. Dinan, "The Physical Consequences of Depressive Illness," *British Medical Journal,* 318 (Mar. 27, 1999), 826.
2. A "Mental Health: A Report of the Surgeon General." Available on the Web site of the National Institute of Mental Health, www.nimh.nih.gov.
3 Sexually abused girls have a very high risk of depression, according to research by Frank Putnam, summarized in *Clinical Psychiatry News,* 19 (Dec. 1991), 3.
4. K. S. Kendler, R. C. Kessler, et al., "Stressful Life Events, Genetic

Liability, and Onset of an Episode of Major Depression in Women," *American Journal of Psychiatry,* 152 (June 1995), 833–42.

5. D. M. Almeida and R. C. Kessler, "Everyday Stressors and Gender Differences in Daily Distress," *Journal of Personality and Social Psychology,* 75 (Sept. 1998), 670–80.

6. M. A. Whooley et al., "Case-finding Instruments for Depression. Two Questions Are as Good as Many," *Journal of General Internal Medicine,* 12 (July 1997), 439–45.

7. J. E. Barrett et al., "The Prevalence of Psychiatric Disorders in a Primary Care Practice," *Archives of General Psychiatry,* 45 (Dec. 1988), 1100–1106.

8. Peter D. Kramer, in *Listening to Prozac* (Penguin, 1997) and the U.S. surgeon general's 1999 report on mental health, cited above, both make the point that the distinction between anxiety and depression may be less strong than has been traditionally conceived.

9. See, for instance, R. C. Shelton et al., "The Undertreatment of Dysthymia," *Journal of Clinical Psychiatry,* 58 (Feb. 1997), 59–65.

10. R. M. Glass, "Treating Depression as a Recurrent or Chronic Disease," *Journal of the American Medical Association,* 281 (Jan. 6, 1999), 83–84.

CHAPTER FOUR: WHAT'S WRONG WITH CONVENTIONAL ANTIDEPRESSANTS?

1. A summary (press release) is available on the Web site of the National Depressive and Manic-Depressive Association, www.ndmda.org.

2. See Dr. Steven Bratman's monograph on St. John's wort at the TNP.com Web site. Dr. Bratman is the medical director of TNP.com, which provides science-based information on natural medicine for consumers and professionals. Also see J. M. Cott JM, "In Vitro Receptor Binding and Enzyme Inhibition by Hypericum Perforatum Extract," *Pharmacopsychiatry,* 30 (Sept. 1997), suppl. 2, 108–112.

CHAPTER FIVE: BEATING DEPRESSION WITH SAM-e

1. G. M. Bressa, "S-adenosyl-l-methionine (SAMe) as Antidepressant: Meta-analysis of Clinical Studies," *Acta Neurologica Scandinavia Supplementum,* 154 (1994), 7–14.

2. K. M. Bell et al., "S-adenosylmethionine Blood Levels in Major Depression: Changes with Drug Treatment," *Acta Neurologica Scandinavia Supplementum,* 154 (1994), 15–18.

3. B. L. Kagan et al., "Oral S-adenosylmethionine in Depression: A Randomized, Double-blind, Placebo-Controlled Trial," *American Journal of Psychiatry,* 147 (May 1990), 591–95 and J. F. Rosenbaum et al., "The Antidepressant Potential of Oral S-adenosyl-L-methionine," *Acta Psychiatry Scandinavia,* 81 (May 1990), 432–36.

4. See, for instance, C. Berlanga et al., "Efficacy of S-adenosyl-L-methionine in Speeding the Onset of Action of Imipramine," *Psychiatry Research,* 44 (Dec. 1992), 257–62.

CHAPTER SIX: THE SECOND ACT: LIFE AFTER DEPRESSION

1. R. W. Larson et al., "Divergent Worlds: The Daily Emotional Experiences of Mothers and Fathers in the Domestic and Public Spheres," *Journal of Personality and Social Psychology,* 67 (Dec. 1994), 1034–46.

2. See, for instance, A. W. Garvin, K. F. Koltyn, and W. P. Morgan, "Influence of Acute Physical Activity and Relaxation on State Anxiety and Blood Lactate in Untrained College Males," *International Journal of Sports Medicine,* 18 (Aug. 1997), 470–76.

3. Presented at the Nov. 1999 meetings in Toronto of the Association for the Advancement of Behavior Therapy.

4. A good summary of two decades' worth of research appears in M. A. Tkachuk and G. L. Martin, "Exercise Therapy for Patients with Psychiatric Disorders: Research and Clinical Implications," *Professional Psychology: Research and Practice,* 30 (June 1999), 275–82.

5. In *Prozac Diary* (Penguin, 1999), Lauren Slater talks about the loss of identity that occurs when symptoms lessen.

CHAPTER SEVEN: THE ACHING JOINTS OF OSTEOARTHRITIS

1. J. K. Rayo et al., "Use of Complementary Therapies for Arthritis among Patients of Rheumatologists," *Annals of Internal Medicine,* 131 (Sept. 21, 1999), 409–16.

2. Quoted in "Stepping Away from OA: A Scientific Conference on the Prevention of Onset, Progression, and Disability of Osteoarthritis," July 23–24, 1999, Bethesda, Md. The conference summary, scientific sessions, is available on the Web site of the National Institute of Arthritis and Musculoskeletal and Skin Diseases, www.nih/gov/niams/reports.

3. C. Cooper et al., "Occupational Activity and Osteoarthritis of the Knee," *Annals of the Rheumatic Diseases* 53 (Feb. 1994), 90–93. Also see D. T. Felson, "Occupational Physical Demands, Knee Bending, and Knee Osteoarthritis: Results from the Framingham Study," *Journal of Rheumatology,* 18 (Oct. 1991), 1587–92.

4. P. Dieppe, "Osteoarthritis: Time to Shift the Paradigm," *British Medical Journal,* 318 (May 15, 1999), 1299–330.

5. D. T. Felson and M. C. Nevitt, "The Effects of Estrogen on Osteoarthritis," *Current Opinion in Rheumatology,* 10 (May 1998), 269–72.

6. C. Slemenda et al., "Reduced Quadriceps Strength Relative to Body Weight: A Risk Factor for Knee Osteoarthritis in Women?" *Arthritis and Rheumatism,* 41 (Nov. 1998), 1951–59.

7. M. J. Shields, "Anti-inflammatory Drugs and Their Effects on Cartilage Synthesis and Renal Function," *European Journal of Rheumatology and Inflammation,* 13 (1993), 7–16.

CHAPTER EIGHT: NATURAL BORN PAINKILLER

1. I. Caruso and V. Pietrogrande, "Italian Double-blind Multicenter Study Comparing S-adenosylmethionine, Naproxen, and Placebo in

the Treatment of Degenerative Joint Disease," *American Journal of Medicine,* 83 (Nov. 1987), suppl. 5A, 66–71.

2. R. Berger and H. Nowak, "A New Medical Approach to the Treatment of Osteoarthritis: Report of an Open Phase IV Study with Ademethionine (Gumbaral)," *American Journal of Medicine,* 83 (Nov. 1987), suppl. 5A, 84–88.

3. The complete statement can be found on the organization's Web site: www.arthritis.org.

4. S. Gutierrez et al., "SAMe Restores the Changes in the Proliferation and in the synthesis of Fibronectin and Proteoglycans Induced by Tumour Necrosis Factor Alpha on Cultured Rabbit Synovial Cells," *British Journal of Rheumatology,* 36 (Jan. 1997), 27–31.

5. A. Maccagno et al., "Double-blind Controlled Clinical Trial of Oral S-adenosylmethionine versus Piroxicam in Knee Osteoarthritis," *American Journal of Medicine,* 83 (Nov. 1987), suppl. 5A, 72–77.

6. B. Konig, "A Long-term (Two Years) Clinical Trial with S-adenosylmethionine for the Treatment of Osteoarthritis," *American Journal of Medicine,* 83 (Nov. 1987), suppl. 5A, 89–94.

7. M. E. van Baar et al., "Effectiveness of Exercise Therapy in Patients with Osteoarthritis of the Hip or Knee: A Systematic Review of Randomized Clinical Trials," *Arthritis and Rheumatology,* 42 (July 1999), 1361–69. For a more readable overview of the subject, see M. A. Minor, "Exercise in the Treatment of Osteoarthritis," *Rheumatic Diseases Clinics of North America,* 25 (May 1999), 397–415.

8. W. H. Ettinger et al., "A Randomized Trial Comparing Aerobic Exercise and Resistance Exercise with a Health Education Program in Older Adults with Knee Osteoarthritis. The Fitness Arthritis and Seniors Trial (FAST)," *Journal of the American Medical Association,* 277 (Jan. 1, 1997), 25–31.

9. D. T. Felson et al., "Weight Loss Reduces the Risk for Symptomatic Knee Osteoarthritis in Women. The Framingham Study," *Annals of Internal Medicine,* 116 (Apr. 1, 1992), 535–39.

10. Reported David Rampe, "Losing Pounds by Surfing, on the Web," *New York Times,* Dec. 7, 1999.

11. M. L. Klem et al., "A Descriptive Study of Individuals Successful at Long-term Maintenance of Substantial Weight-Loss," *American Journal of Clinical Nutrition,* 66 (Aug. 1997), 239–46.

12. For a thorough explication of the food allergy hypothesis, see Dr. Neal Barnard, *Foods That Fight Pain* (Harmony Books, 1998).

13. T. E. McAlindon, "Do Antioxidant Micronutrients Protect against the Development and Progression of Knee Osteoarthritis?" *Arthritis and Rheumatism,* 39 (Apr. 1996), 648–56.

14. T. E. McAlindon et al., "Relation of Dietary Intake and Serum Levels of Vitamin D to Progression of Osteoarthritis of the Knee among Participants in the Framingham Study," *Annals of Internal Medicine,* 125 (Sept. 1, 1996), 353–59; and N. E. Lane et al., "Serum Vitamin D Levels and the Incident Changes of Radiographic Hip Osteoarthritis: A Longitudinal Study. Study of Osteoporotic Fractures Group," *Arthritis and Rheumatism,* 42 (May 1999), 854–60.

15. Cited in "Stepping Away from OA: A Scientific Conference on the Prevention of Onset, Progression, and Disability of Osteoarthritis," public session, July 24, 1999, Bethesda, Md. The conference summary, scientific and public sessions, is available on the Web site of the National Institute of Arthritis and Musculoskeletal and Skin Diseases, www.nih/gov/niams/reports.

16. J. Y. Reginster et al., "Glucosamine Sulfate Significantly Reduces Progression of Knee Osteoarthritis over Three Years: A Large, Randomized, Placebo-controlled, Double-blind, Prospective Trial," presented at the 1999 Annual Scientific Meetings of the American College of Rheumatology. An abstract is available at the organization's Web site: www.rheumatology.org.

CHAPTER NINE: NEW HOPE FOR FIBROMYALGIA SUFFERERS

1. F. Wolfe, J. Anderson, D. Harkness, et al., "Health Status and Disease Severity in Fibromyalgia: Results of a Six-Center Longitudinal Study," *Arthritis and Rheumatism,* 40 (Sept. 1997), 1571–79. The more hopeful study is G. Granges, P. Zilko, and G. O. Littlejohn, "Fibromyalgia Syndrome: Assessment of the Severity of the Condi-

tion Two Years after Diagnosis," *Journal of Rheumatology,* 21 (1994), 523–29.

2. D. L. Goldenberg, "Fibromyalgia Syndrome a Decade Later: What Have We Learned?" *Archives of Internal Medicine,* 159 (Apr. 26, 1999), 777–85. This article provides a good summary of the effectiveness of different treatment protocols. The two-step treatment is presented in D. Goldenberg, M. Mayskiy, C. Mossey, et al., "A Randomized, Double-blind Crossover Trial of Fluoxetine and Amitriptyline in the Treatment of Fibromyalgia," *Arthritis and Rheumatism,* 39 (Nov. 1996), 1852–59.

3. A. Tavoni, C. Vitali, A. Bombardieri, and G. Pasero, "Evaluation of S-adenosylmethionine in Primary Fibromyalgia: A Double-blind Crossover Study," *American Journal of Medicine,* 83 (Nov. 20, 1987), suppl. 5A, 107–10; S. Jacobsen, B. Danneskiold-Samsoe, R. B. Andersen, "Oral S-adenosylmethionine in Primary Fibromyalgia, Double-blind Clinical Evaluation," *Scandinavian Journal of Rheumatology* 20 (1991), 294–302; H. Volkmann, J. Norregaard, S. Jacobsen, et al., "Double-blind, Placebo-controlled Crossover Study of Intravenous S-adenosyl-L-methionine in Patients with Fibromyalgia," *Scandinavian Journal of Rheumatology,* 26 (1997), 206–11.

4. B. M. Berman, J. P. Swyers, "Complementary Medicine Treatments for Fibromyalgia Syndrome," *Baillieres Best Practice and Research Clinical Rheumatology,* 13 (Sept. 1999), 487–92.

5. *Dr. Andrew Weil's Self-Healing,* May 1996, has some encouraging case studies.

CHAPTER TEN: SAM-e FOR LIVER DISORDERS, AND OTHER PROMISING RESEARCH

1. S.R. Paredes et al., "Beneficial Effect of S-adenosyl-L-methionine in Lead Intoxication. Another Approach to Clinical Therapy," *International Journal of Biochemistry,* 17 (1985), 625–29; and S. R. Paredes et al., "S-adenosyl-L-methionine and Lead Intoxication: Its Therapeutic Effect Varying the Route of Administration," *Ecotoxicology and Environmental Safety,* 12 (Dec. 1986), 252–60.

2. M. Frezza et al., "Reversal of Intrahepatic Cholestatis of Pregnancy in Women after High Dose S-adenosyl-L-methionine Administration," *Hepatology* 1984 Mar.–Apr.; 4(2): 274–78; P. L. Nicastri et al., "A Randomised Placebo-controlled Trial of Ursodeoxycholic Acid and S-adenosylmethionine in the Treatment of Intrahepatic Cholestasis of Pregnancy," *British Journal of Obstetrics and Gynecology,* 105 (Nov. 1998), 1205–1207.

3. M. Frezza et al., "High Blood Alcohol Levels in Women. The Role of Decreased Gastric Alcohol Dehydrogenase Activity and First-pass Metabolism," *New England Journal of Medicine,* 322 (Jan. 11, 1990), 95–99.

4. Z. Hrubec and G. S. Omenn, "Evidence of Genetic Predisposition to Alcoholic Cirrhosis and Psychosis: Twin Concordances for Alcoholism and Its Biological End Points by Zygosity among Male Veterans," *Alcoholism, Clinical and Experimental Research,* 5 (Spring 1981), 207–15.

5. C. Cabrero et al., "Specific Loss of the High-molecular-weight Form of S-adenosyl-L-methionine Synthetase in Human Liver Cirrhosis," *Hepatology,* 8 (Nov.–Dec. 1988), 1530–34.

6. C. S. Lieber et al., "S-adenosyl-L-methionine Attenutates Alcohol-induced Liver Injury in the Baboon," *Hepatology,* (Feb. 1990), 165–72.

7. J. M. Mato et al., "S-adenosylmethionine in Alcoholic Liver Cirrhosis: A Randomized, Placebo-controlled, Double-blind, Multicenter Clinical Trial," *Journal of Hepatology,* 30 (June 1999), 1081–89.

8. Dr. Bratman's monograph on SAM-e appears in the professionals section in TNP.com.

9. L. D. Morrison et al., "Brain S-adenosylmethionine Levels Are Severely Decreased in Alzheimer's Disease," *Journal of Neurochemistry,* 67 (Sept. 1996), 1328–31; T. Bottiglieri et al., "The Clinical Potential of Ademetionine (S-adenosylmethionine) in Neurological Disorders," *Drugs,* 48 (Aug. 1994), 137–52; and L. Parentti et al., "Role of Homocysteine in Age-related Vascular and Nonvascular Diseases," *Aging (Milano),* 9 (Aug. 1997), 241–57.

10. W. O. Shekim et al., "S-adenosyl-L-methionine (SAM) in Adults with ADHD, RS: Preliminary Results from an Open Trial," *Psychopharmacology Bulletin,* 26 (1990), 249–53; and G. Gatto et al., "Analgezing Effect of a Methyl Donor (S-adenosylmethionine) in Migraine: an Open Clinical Trial," *International Journal of Clinical Pharmacology Research,* 6 (1986), 15–17.

11. R. Surtees and K. Hyland. "Cerebrospinal Fluid Concentrations of S-adenosylmethionine, Methionine, and 5-methyltetrahydrofolate in a Reference Population: Cerebrospinal Fluid S-adenosylmethionine Declines with Age in Humans," *Biochemical Medicine and Metabolic Biology,* 44 (Oct. 1990), 192–99.

12. C. Cimino et al., "Age-related Modification of Dopaminergic and Beta-adrenergic Receptor System: Restoration to Normal Activity by Modifying Membrane Fluidity with S-adenosylmethionine," *Life Sciences,* 34 (May 21, 1984), 2029–39.

CHAPTER ELEVEN: HOW TO TAKE SAM-e

1. D. M. Eisenberg, R. C. Kessler, et al., "Unconventional Medicine in the United States. Prevalence, Costs, and Patterns of Use," *New England Journal of Medicine,* 328 (Jan. 28, 1993), 246–52.

2. D. M. Eisenberg et al., "Trends in Alternative Medicine Use in the United States, 1990–1997: Results of a Follow-up National Survey," *Journal of the American Medical Association,* 280 (Nov. 11, 1998), 1569–75.

CHAPTER TWELVE: A SHOPPER'S GUIDE TO SAM-e

1. Results are available at www.consumerlab.com.

2. The editorial appeared in the Apr. 1999 issue of *Alternative Medicine Review* (Page 73).

3. *Good Housekeeping Institute's testing:* The complete findings appear in Catherine Heusel, "Hot Natural Remedies," *Good Housekeeping,* Mar. 2000.

INDEX